MARILYN HENRION

Noise

September 30- October 25, 2008

"The isle is full of noises,
Sounds and sweet airs, that give delight, and hurt not.
Sometimes a thousand twangling instruments
Will hum about mine ears; and sometimes voices,
That, if I then had waked after long sleep,
Will make me sleep again."

Shakespeare, The Tempest

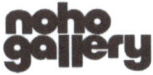

530 West 25 Street, New York, NY 10001   (212)367-7063

ISBN 13: 978-1479156474
ISBN 10: 1479156477

www.marilynhenrion.com   marilynhenrion@mac.com   (917)359-4621

Photo credits: D. James Dee

Cover: Red White & Blue, detail

INTRODUCTION

In this series of works, the artist celebrates noise as a metaphor for life. ...... from the presence of vast interstellar matter that fills the universe to the activity of billions of quantum particles contained in every cell in our bodies. Noise of thunder. Noise of ocean waves. Noise of a lover's voice. Noise in the spaces between words. Noise of a baby's cry. Noise of a symphony. Noise of our breathing. All reasons to wake up in the morning!

After beginning her artistic career as a painter, Marilyn Henrion chose textiles as her preferred medium in 1975 and never looked back. Having built an international reputation for her exquisitely quilted artworks, the artist now brings her contemporary sensibilities and obsessive hand work to yet another traditional form of textile-based art. In these works, derived from rug hooking techniques, the geometric abstraction which has always characterized her art has been pared down to a minimalism brought to life by the depth of surface inherent in this new format. The controlled serenity of the spare visual elements finds its counterpoint in the raw energy of the surface textures.

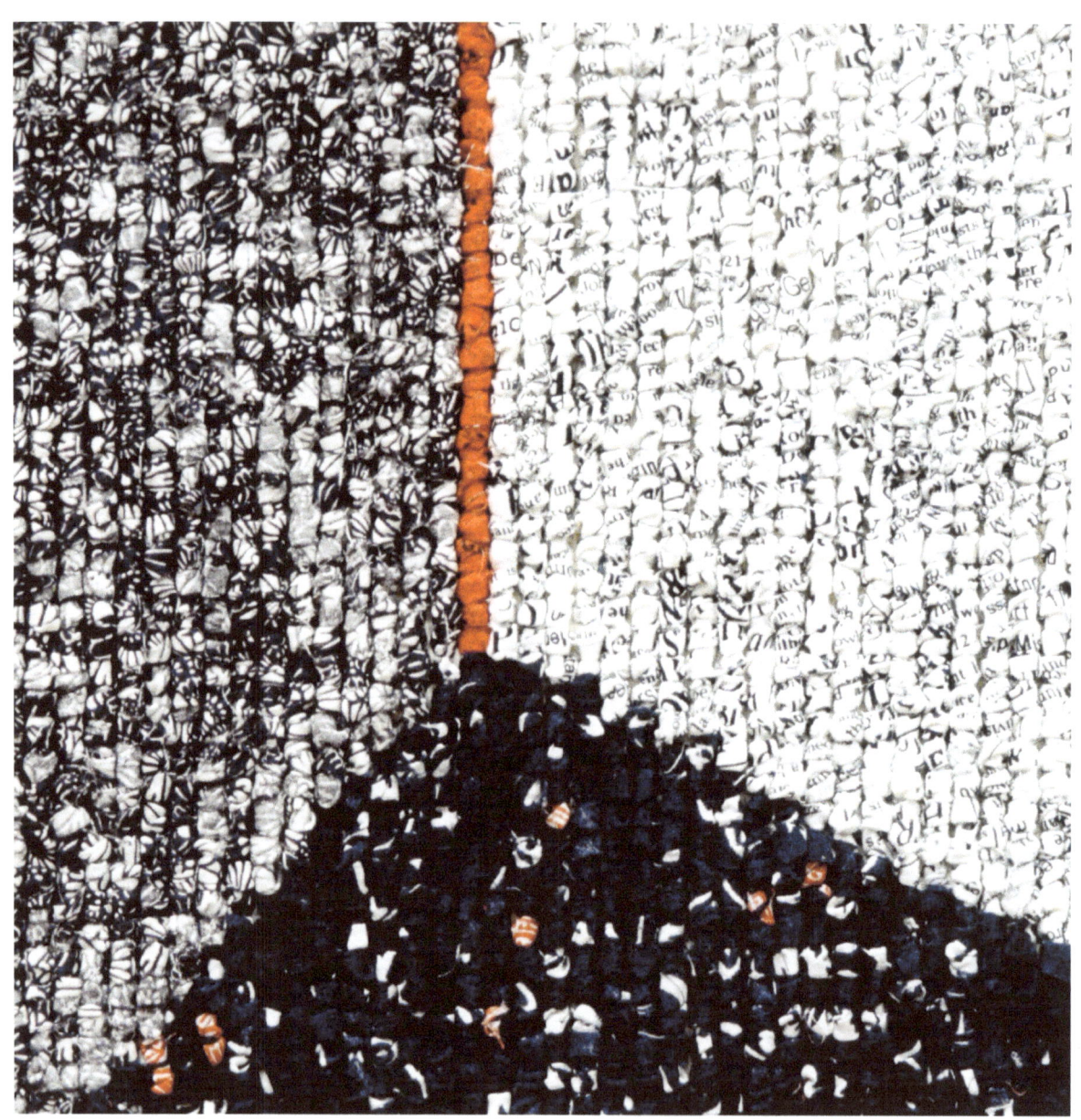

Triad #3 detail   cotton and linen

Marilyn Henrion: A New Music of the Rectangles and Spheres

Essay by Ed McCormack

Only an extraordinary sense of conviction could make an established artist at mid-career willfully adopt a technique that all but the most savvy viewers will almost automatically associate with industrial design rather than fine art, as Marilyn Henrion does in her "Noise" series, and then proceed to invest it with an artistic authority that subverts all expectations. Henrion has been persistently surprising us since 1975, when she switched mediums from painting to textiles and immediately demonstrated that what many still regarded as women's busywork could be a vehicle for sophisticated artistic expression. Since she had been associated with the Beat Generation poets and an active participant of the avant garde Happenings scene in the 1960s, Henrion's change of mediums, which coincided with the rise of the feminist movement, could have seemed incongruous. However, while there was never any question as to her own feminist consciousness, it was her emphasis on formal rather than political issues that made her work endure over subsequent decades. More than a mere gesture of solidarity with the unsung woman quiltmakers who created one of America's great folk art forms, her choice of medium proceeded from an abiding belief that fiber art was a frontier whose serious artistic possibilities had yet to be fully explored.

Unlike the artists of the Pattern and Decoration movement who would follow her lead in 1980s, Henrion never appeared especially beholden to Islamic, Celtic, or other non-Western modes of ornamentation, even while acknowledging the influence of Indian miniatures and Japanese kesa robes on her work. Nor did she seem unduly concerned with challenging the longstanding taboo against decoration in fine art. Rather, she employed quilting and other fiber art techniques to create works that, by virtue of her command of pure form and color, demanded to be considered within the context of mainstream geometric abstraction.

The question of context was settled all the more vehemently by Henrion's careful designation of her works as "hand pieced and stitched constructions", instead of "art-quilts" or any of the other terms all too often employed to relegate certain types of work by woman artists to the ghetto of the artsy craftsy. None of which is to imply that she did not exploit the tactile and coloristic opulence peculiar to her medium to the fullest. Indeed, few painters could match the synthesis of formal austerity and surface sensuality that she achieved by combining variously textured fabrics, from matte to silken, with reflective metallic brocades and hand-stitching that produced puckers and pulls as subtlety individualistic as brushstrokes.

Henrion proved that fiber art could not only compete with painting in terms of formal power and aesthetic delectation, but that it could also carry as much emotional impact -- particularly in her 2005 "Disturbances" series, in which architectonic abstract forms swerved from their geometric moorings in a manner that viscerally evoked the terrorist attacks on the Twin Towers. But while she tapped into a particularly powerful communal trauma in that series, she is better known for works whose primary appeal is the pure visual pleasure that they provide. (No wonder she loves Matisse, who was influenced by growing up in Bohain, a province of France renowned for its weavers of elegant, colorful fabrics not unlike those that have served so successfully as her own working palette.)

Perhaps the most radical aspect of Henrion's newest pieces, then, is her deliberate eschewal of the immediately ingratiating qualities that have always made her compositions so seductive. In contrast to the Byzantine complexity, baroque swirls, and bright primaries enhanced by gold and silver brocades in her earlier works, these sparer geometric compositions call upon a different tradition of textile based art, derived from rug-making, which she refers to as "cotton and linen textile construction". The tactile yet uniform surface, achieved by a process of hooking strips of fabric into a mesh canvas foundation to produce an overall texture of more or less even

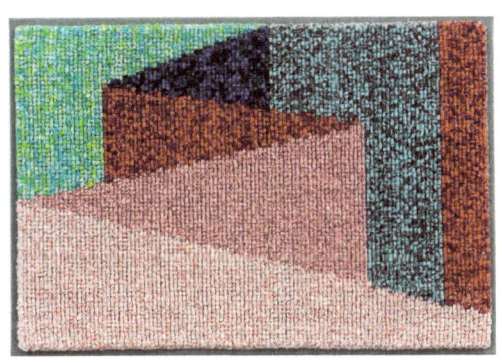

nubs, provides Henrion with the perfect context for forms which are considerably more pared down and minimalist than her previous ones. And that these forms are actually woven directly into the fabric to create the composition, rather than stitched together in the manner of collage, lends them a different kind of depth and sensuousness.

Despite its name, Henrion's "Noise" series is paradoxically "quieter" than her hand pieced and stitched constructions. In contrast to the fanfare of rioting patterns, textures, and colors in those earlier pieces, these new ones, with their softer secondary colors subtly modulated by particles of variegated hues, suggest a more muted chromatic cacophony, prompted by Henrion's reading of the lines in Shakespeare's "The Tempest" that go: "The isle is full of noises, / Sounds and sweet airs, that give delight, and hurt not. / Sometimes a thousand twangling instruments / Will hum about mine ears; and sometimes voices, / That, if I then had waked after long sleep, / Will make me sleep again".

Indeed, while Henrion employs color with greater restraint and subtlety than ever before, in a manner as "painterly" and harmonically complex in its in its own way as a Jules Olitski or a Darby Bannard, her new works suggest a commingling of sounds akin to the steady hum of "white noise", evoking, as the artist herself puts it, everything 'from the presence of vast interstellar matter that

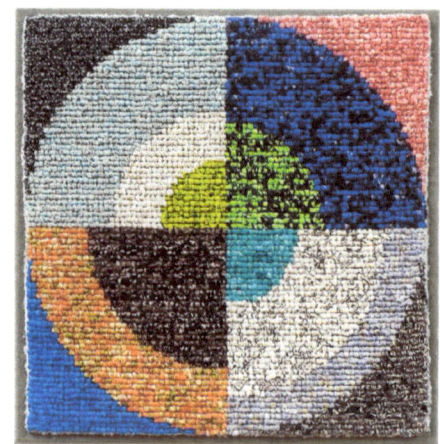

fills the universe to the activity of billions of quantum particles contained in every cell of our bodies". Never one to shy away from ambitious subjects-- and what could be more ambitious than echoing visually what amounts to the very Music of the Spheres?

Henrion finds new challenges in encapsulating

profound complexity in a more concentrated geometric context. Her "Meditation #2", for example, with its central circle dissected into four rectangular areas containing smaller misaligned circles of various colors, seems akin to the work of Hilda AF Klint, a Swedish contemporary of Kandinsky, who, like him, saw abstract painting as a path to spiritual exploration, but was never properly acknowledged as one of the true pioneers of modern art.

Whether Henrion is even familiar with Klint, given the earlier artist"s relative obscurity, seems a moot point, since such kinships transcend time and logic, perhaps proving that mysterious spiritual connections play a larger part than we know in the evolution of aesthetic tendencies and ideas. Conscious or not, in another cotton and linen textile construction by Henrion called "Quartet", one can likewise discern a stylistic empathy with the paintings of

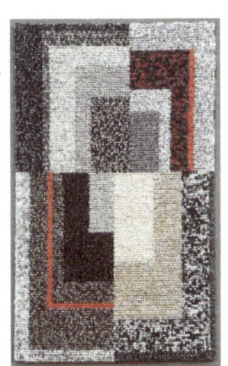

Irene Rice Pereira, who had the double misfortune of being a woman and being a geometric painter when the art scene was dominated by the macho bully boys of "Action Painting". Not only does "Quartet's" composition of interlocking rectangles and a mostly monochrome palette of subtle gray tones, relieved here and there by spare areas of red, remind one of Pereira, but the particulate textures of the wool in Henrion's work appear to channel her distinctive stippling technique. Such tributes to earlier women artists whose significance has been overlooked by phallocentric art historians seem auspiciously in keeping with the ethos of an artist who, for all her insistence on aesthetic autonomy, made her feminist sympathies manifest the minute she switched

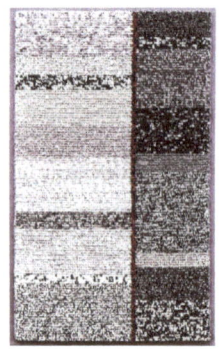

from painting to fiber art.

As always in Henrion's case, however, formal concerns come even more prominently into play, such as the eternal tension between implied perspective and the sanctity of the two-dimensional picture plane seen in the "Noise" series. In works such as "Rift", where a vertical red band unevenly divides variegated areas of gray that suggest visual static on a video screen, and "Strata", which is as rectangularly-based and flatly matter-of-fact as a Mondrian, two-dimensional space clearly triumphs. However, the triangular bias of the numbered compositions that share the title "Vanishing Point" plays with spatial ambiguity, and another grouping of works called "Unfolding" revels more overtly in illusion through Henrion's handling of angularly unfurling, undulating shapes.

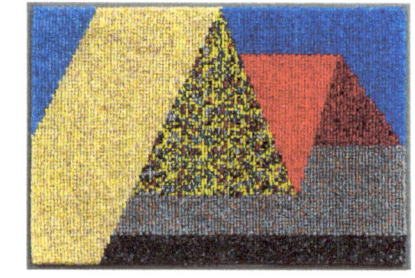

Among the latter works, "Unfolding 2" is especially noteworthy for the artist's reintroduction of brilliant primary hues which restore a familiar chromatic lushness to her new compositional austerity, creating a dynamic synthesis that makes one eager to discover where the ever-evolving art of Marilyn Henrion will go next.

Ed McCormack

Gallery & Studio

New York City, 2008

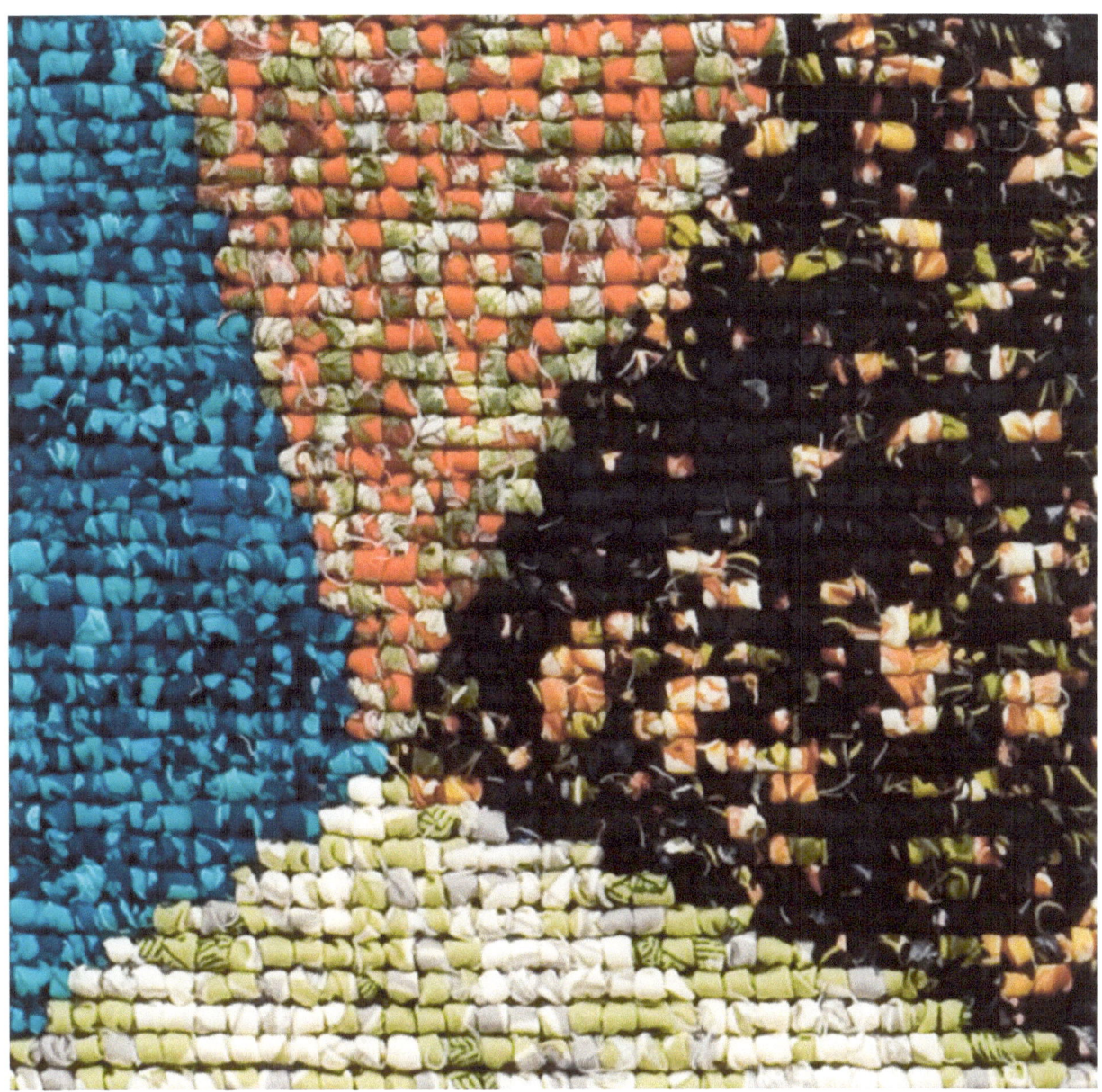

Crossroads, detail

NOISE: Visual, Tactile, Auditory

Essay by Janet Koplos

The critic Clement Greenberg once described a certain kind of abstraction as "homeless representation." By that he meant a visual construction that hints at places or things we know but does not resolve into a picture. That margin between familiar and unfamiliar describes Marilyn Henrion's textile works, both her former visually allusive pieced compositions and her new hooked works. Her last exhibition, "Disturbances," subjected conventional shapes to whirlpool distortions or fun-house mirror warping. Earlier bodies of work fractured architectural elements such as arcades. In the newest pieces, circles float, diagonals converge and rectangles are offset in a happy clatter of geometry.

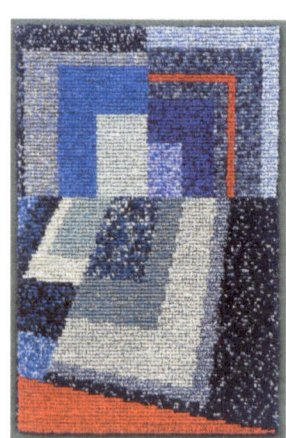

That she has chosen to call this exhibition "Noise," however, seems less justified by the abrupt meeting of shapes than by tiny details of color and texture that her newly chosen method offers, because she employs narrow strips of print fabrics. These strips are compressed as they are worked into a mesh backing, so the print motifs are unidentifiable, registering only as changes in color. Thus the surfaces of Henrion's works are inflected by a speckling that once was familiar to viewers of black and white television screens. The association is strongest in her compositions of those hues and in expanses of frizzled blue as well. But this visual effect, also equivalent to aural static, is in fact constant throughout the various colors and configurations, and acts as a kind of fizz bubbling out of the otherwise well-behaved and orderly shapes.

Consider her systems: square or rectangular formats, interior lines that echo the regular perimeter, or repetitive bands in parallel or concentric formations (as in the Meditations). The surface static works to soften that structure, dissolving the sharp contrasts. In fact, undermining order is almost a constant in Henrion's work; she seems to provide an overall plan only to work against it in other respects. The nine panels of Triads, for instance, are squares subdivided into three parts, not the easy quadrants or diagonal halves that would yield

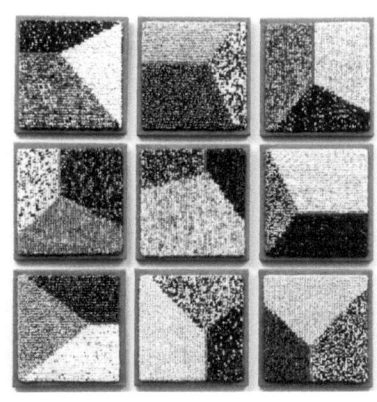

matching triangles. Of the 27 parts, only two appear to be complete triangles; the rest are irregular polygons. Each panel includes one straight border between these parts, perpendicular to its outside edge, while the rest are diagonals. That straight line, a different length in each panel, is a shaft of red-orange amid the differing mixes of black and white. The consequence is that the viewer's eye can't rest when looking at Triads. The shapes and the small but intense lines of color seem to rotate, fold, flop, shift.

Here, and likewise in the eight rectangular panels called Vanishing Points, the viewer repeatedly follows possible lines of relationship and connection without finding an answer that would make this "homeless representation" more at home. Space is implied by the very title, and in each panel, triangular forms come to a point, like a perspective rendering of distance. But there is more than one point, or color moves across the implied space, creating a science-fictiony, mind-bending shift.

Henrion continues to subscribe to the optical illusions that belong to quilting composition. She also links to Modernist abstract painting (recalling artists from Delaunay to Johns and Kelly to Riley)—a circular relationship, since painting has been known to borrow from textile traditions. To the formal qualities of abstract painting she adds the visual softness of frayed edges and the chromatic complexity of printed fabrics, creating artworks that have an appealing hand, show the strategies of a perceptive eye, and evoke an experience of the ear.

Janet Koplos

Senior Editor, Art In America

New York City, 2008

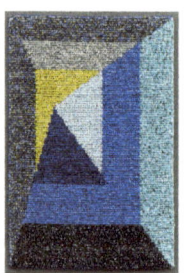 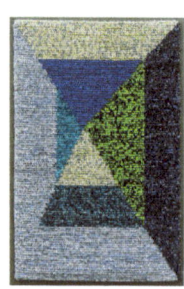 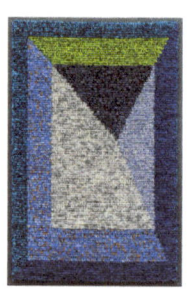 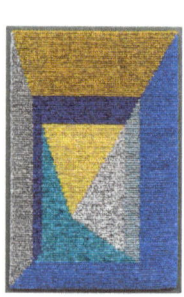

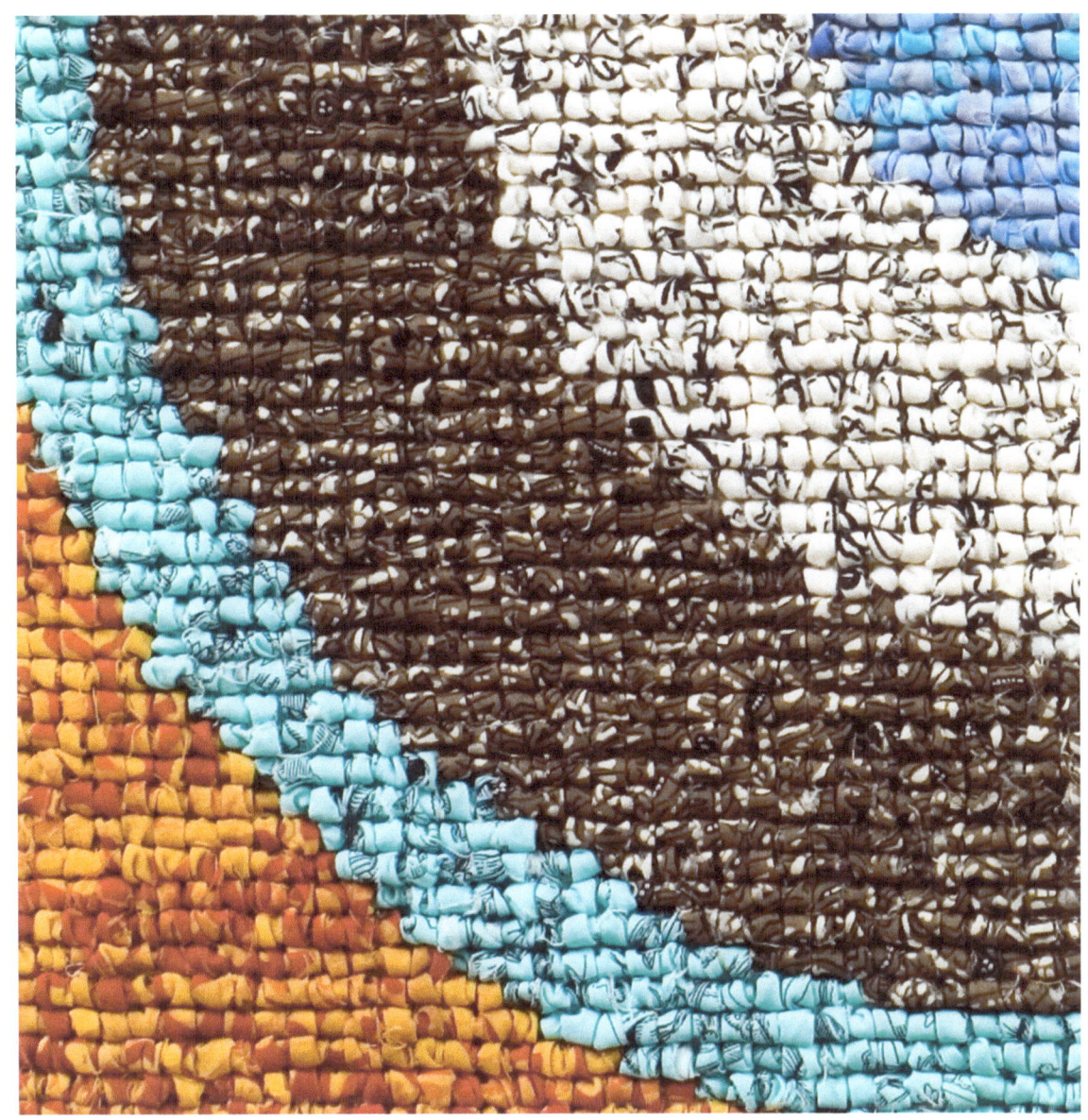

Meditation 4   detail

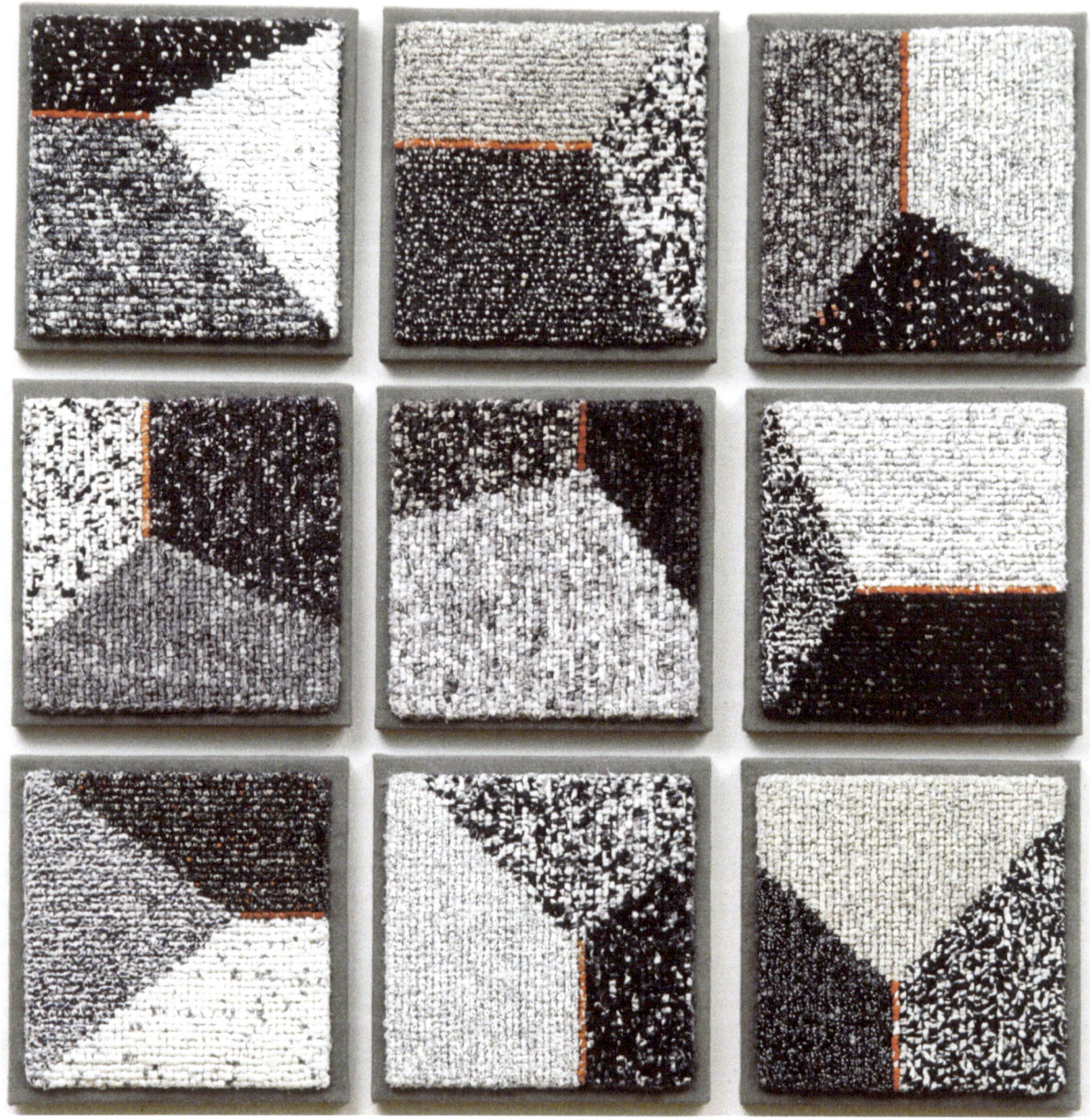

Triads   cotton and linen   nine panels, each 12"x12"   2007

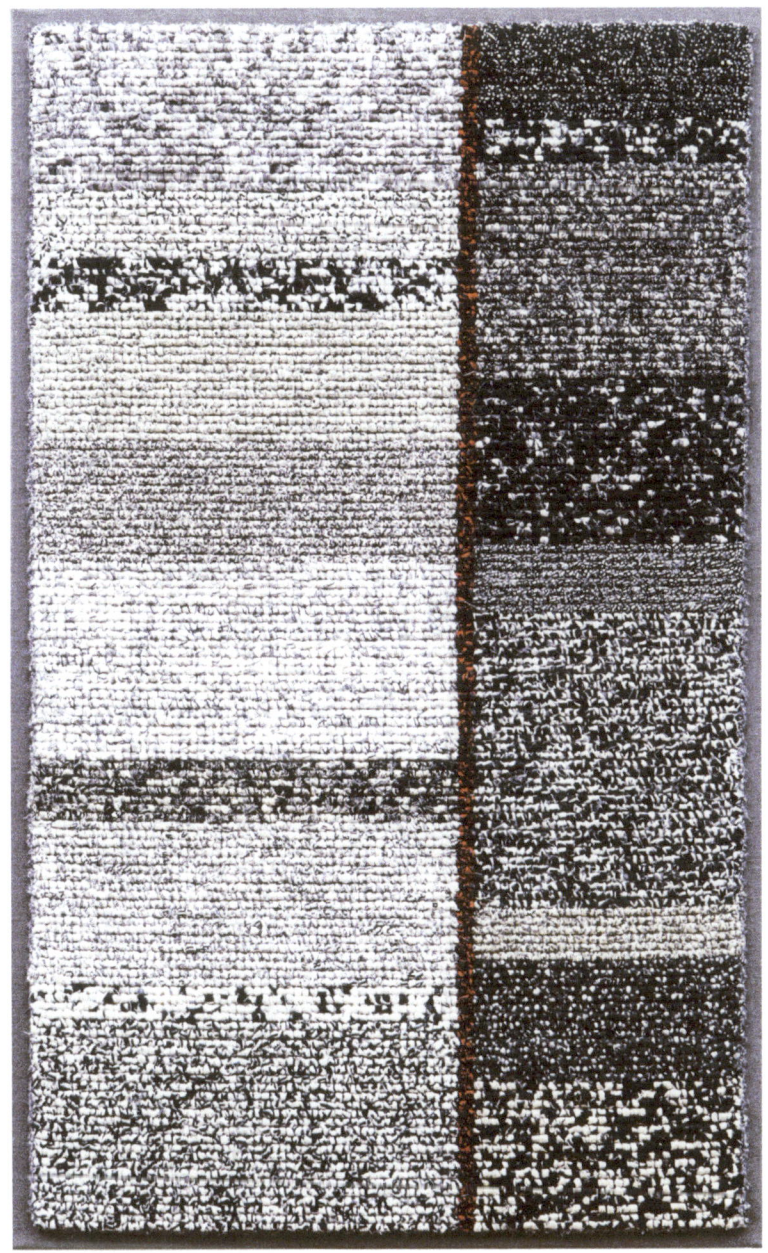

Rift   cotton and linen   31"x21"   2007

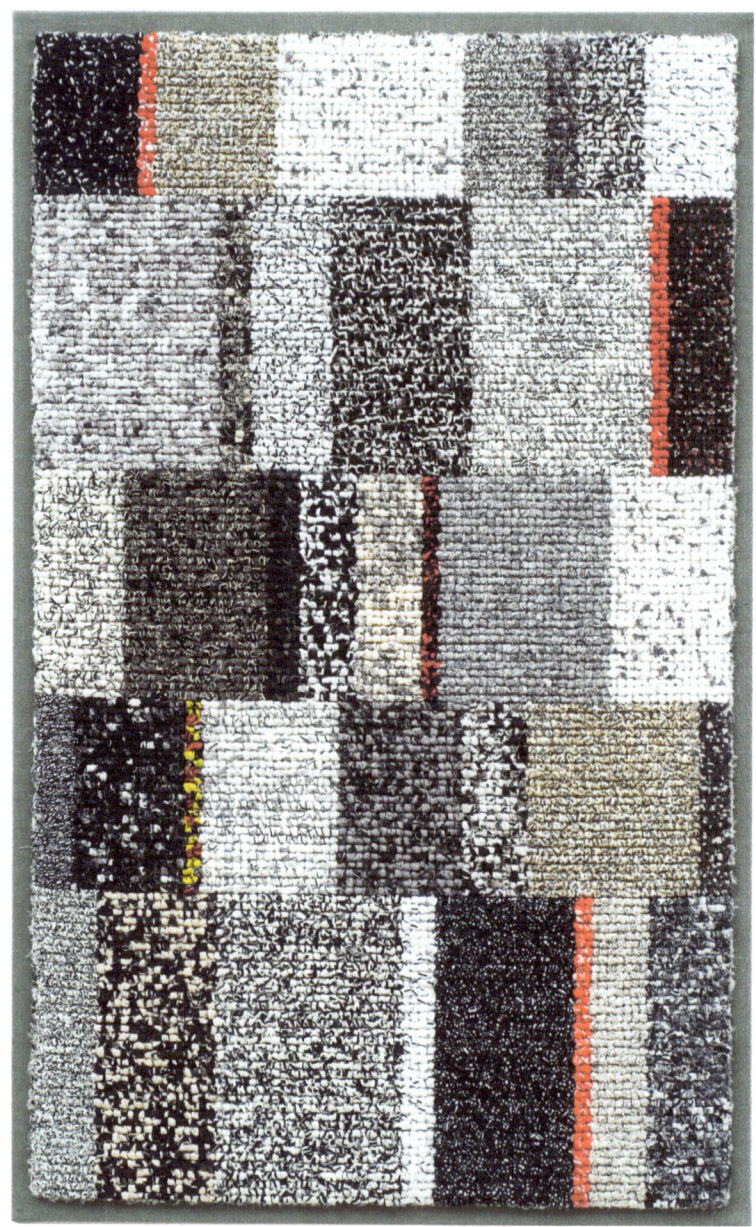

Strata   cotton and linen   38"x24'   2007

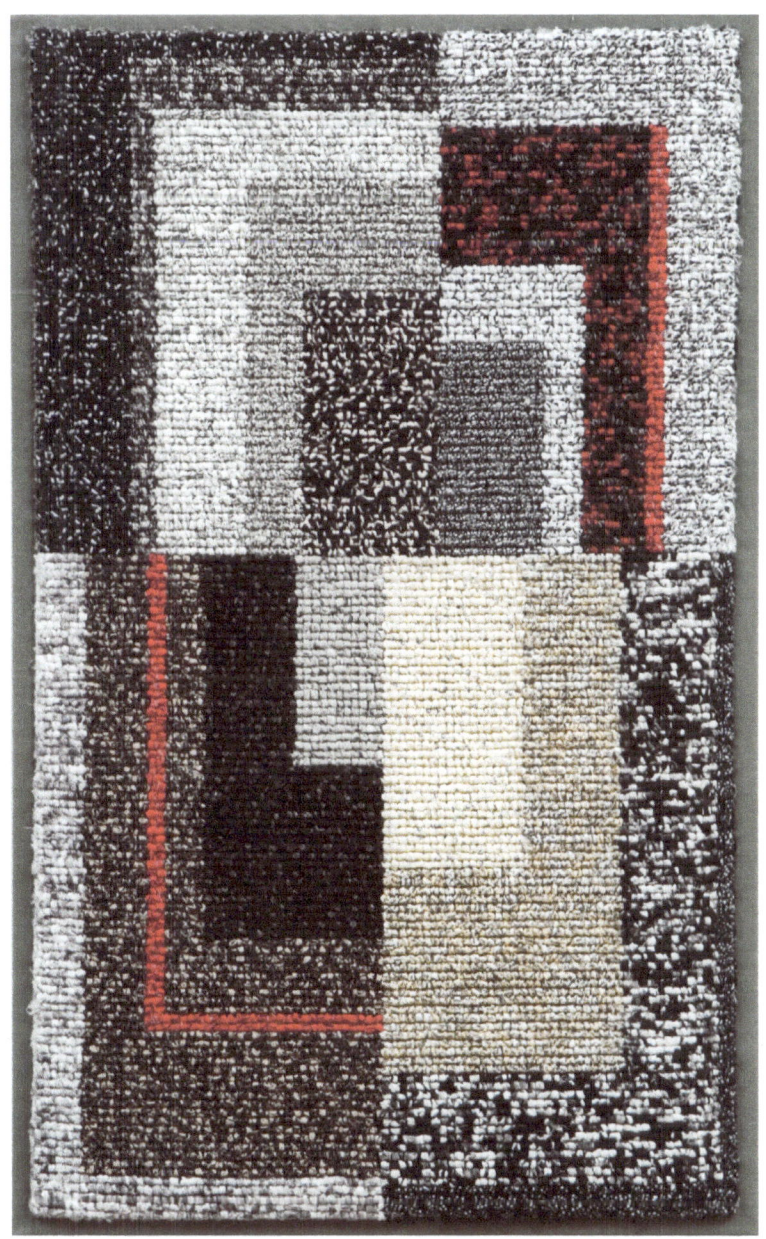

Quartet   cotton and linen   38"x24"   2007

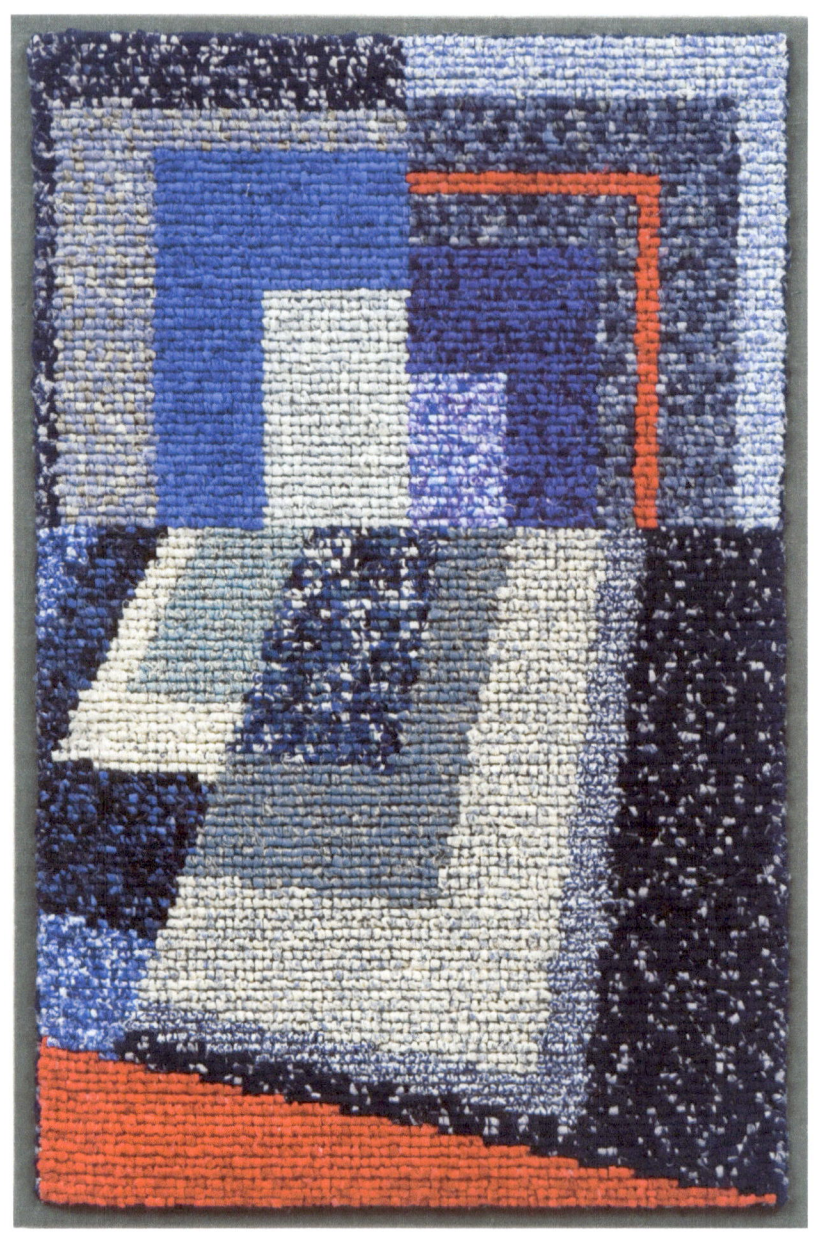

Pandora's Box   cotton and linen   31"x21"   2007

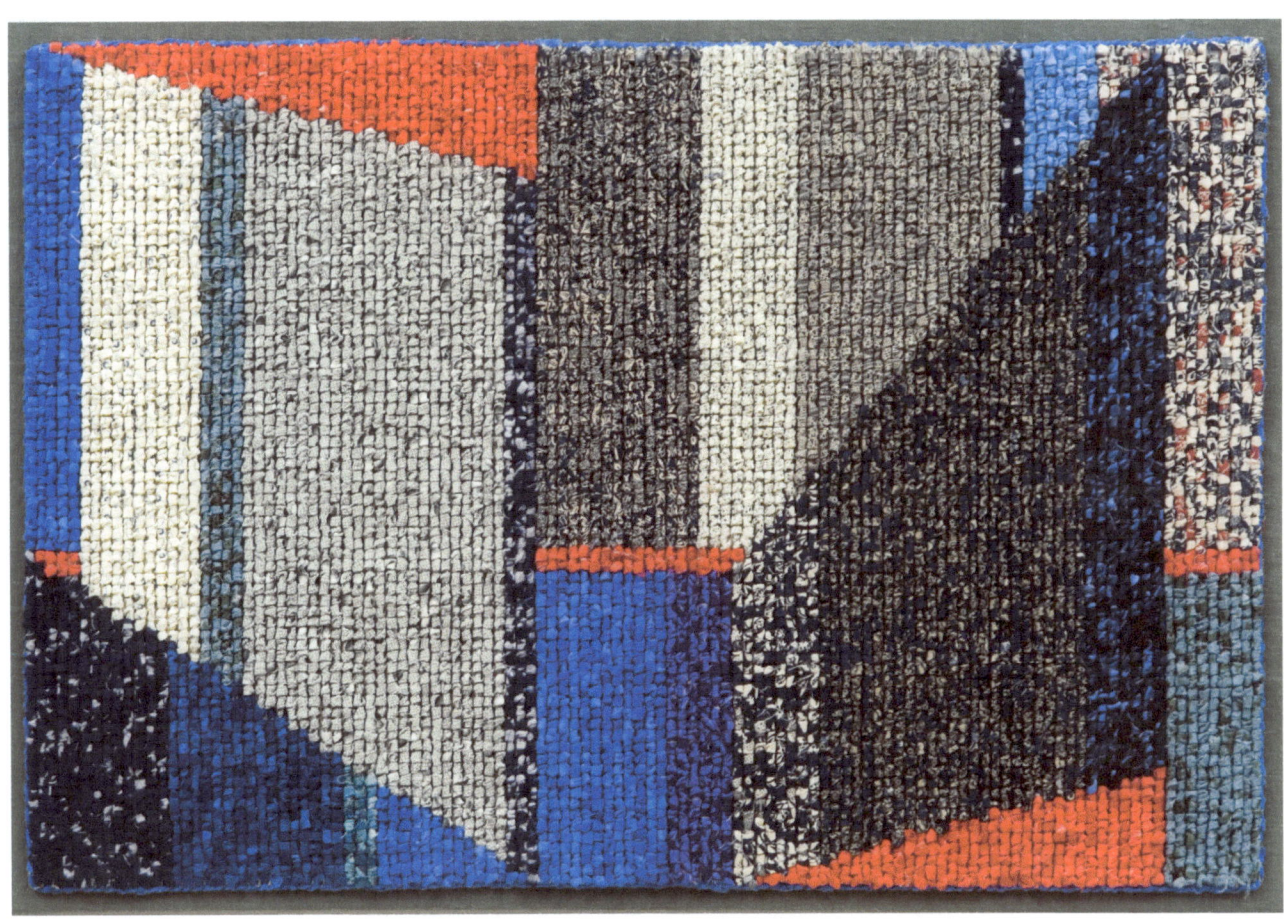

Corridors   cotton and linen   21"x31"   2007

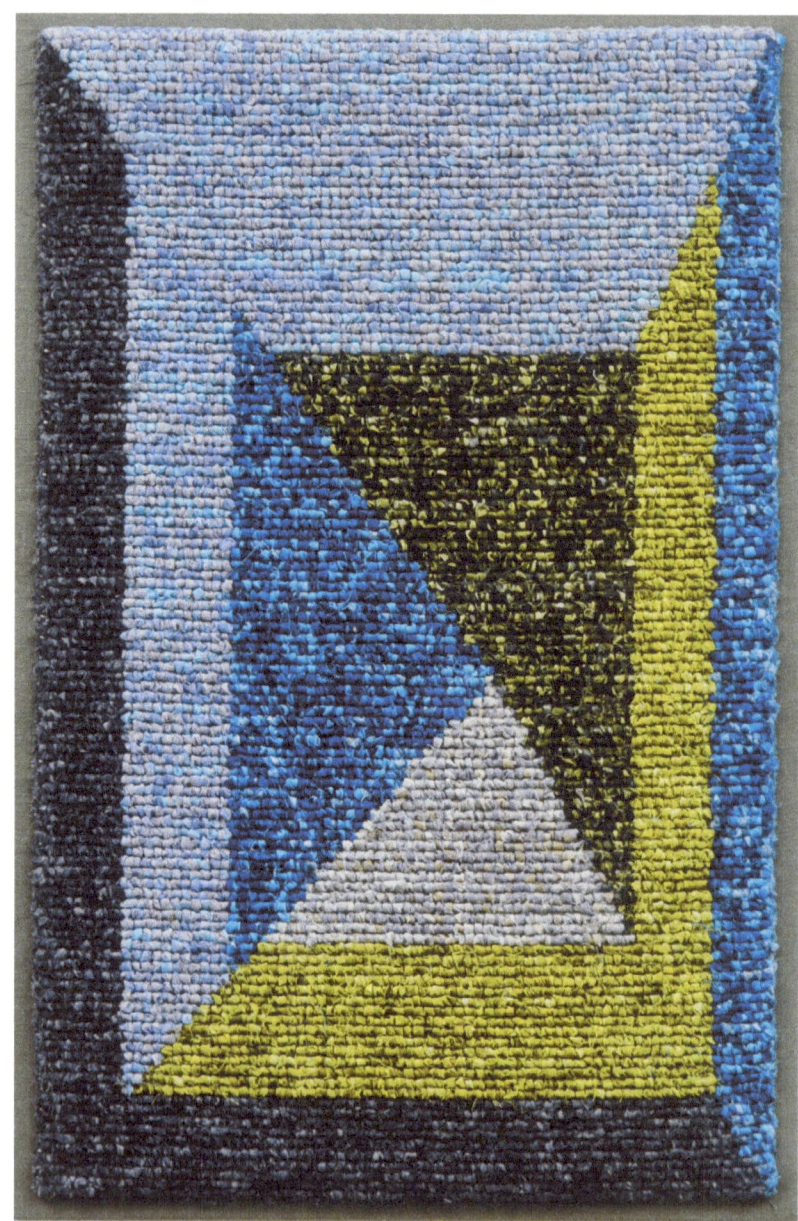

Vanishing Point 1   cotton and linen   31"x21"   2007

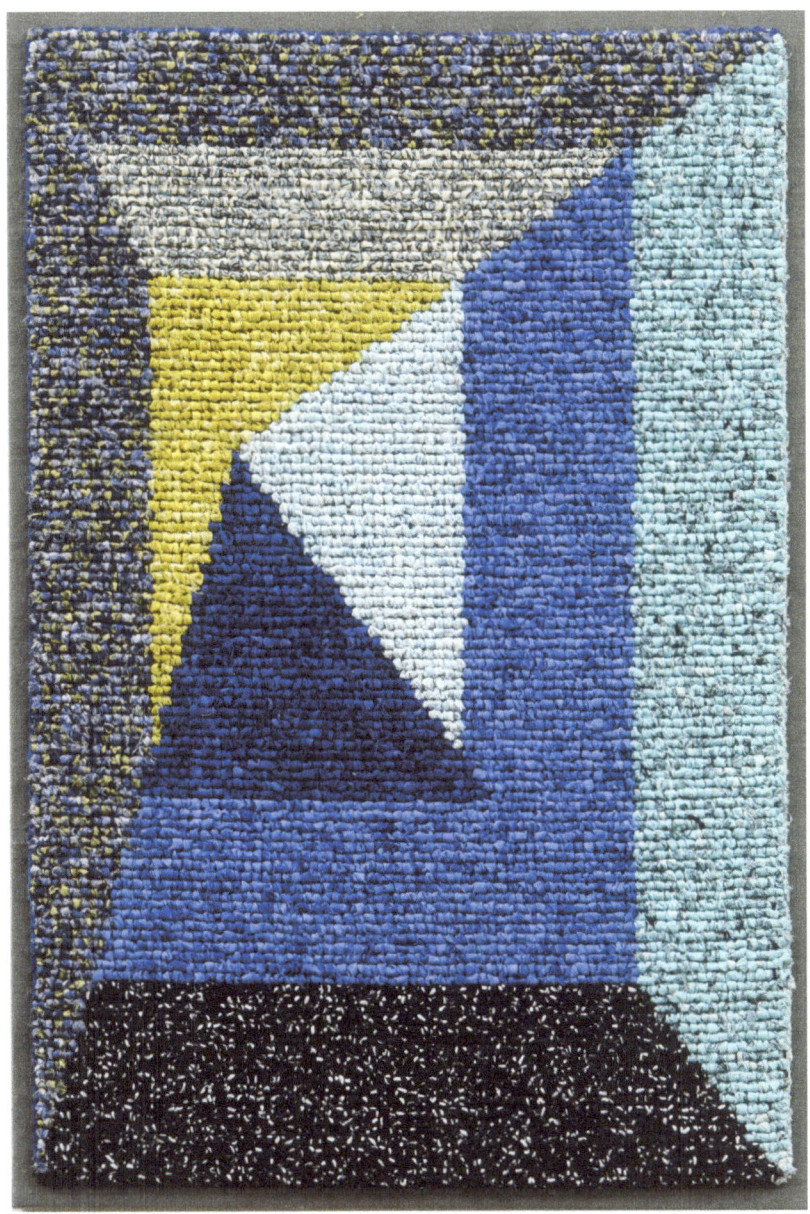

Vanishing Point 2   cotton and linen   31"x21"   2007

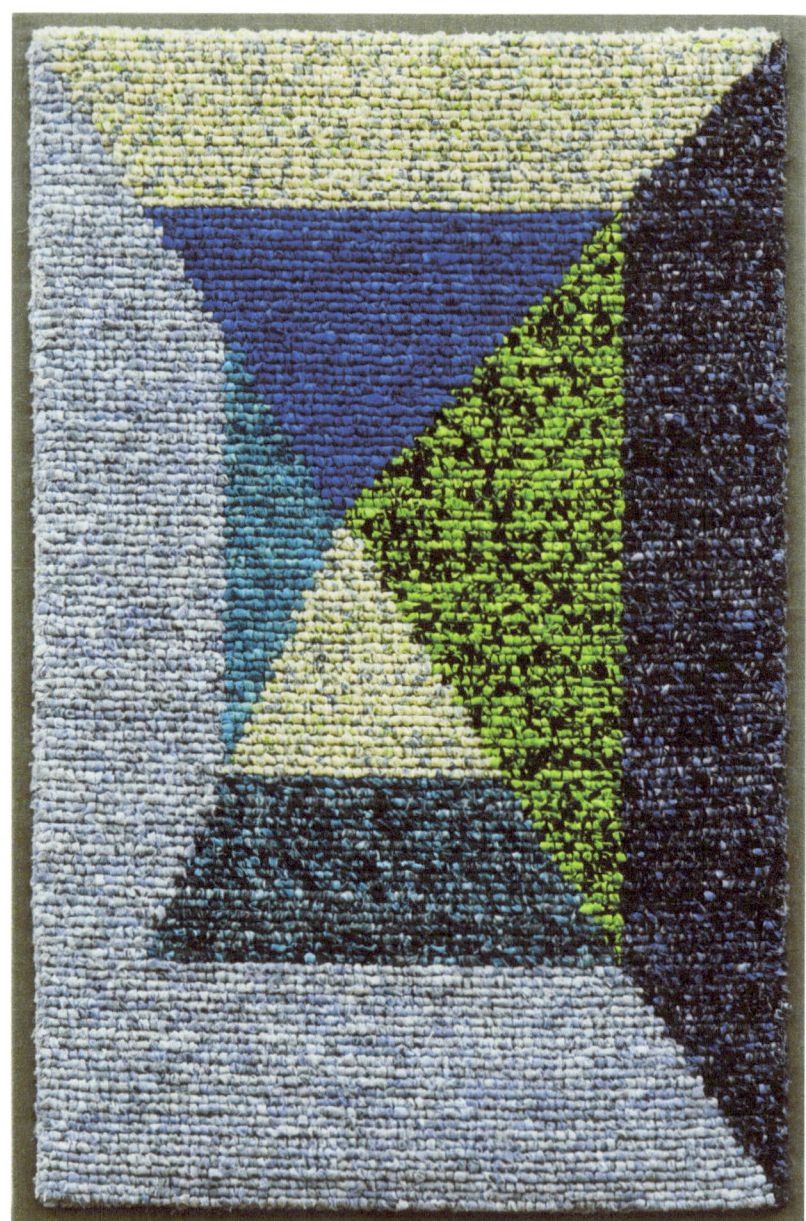

Vanishing Point 3   cotton and linen   31"x21"   2007

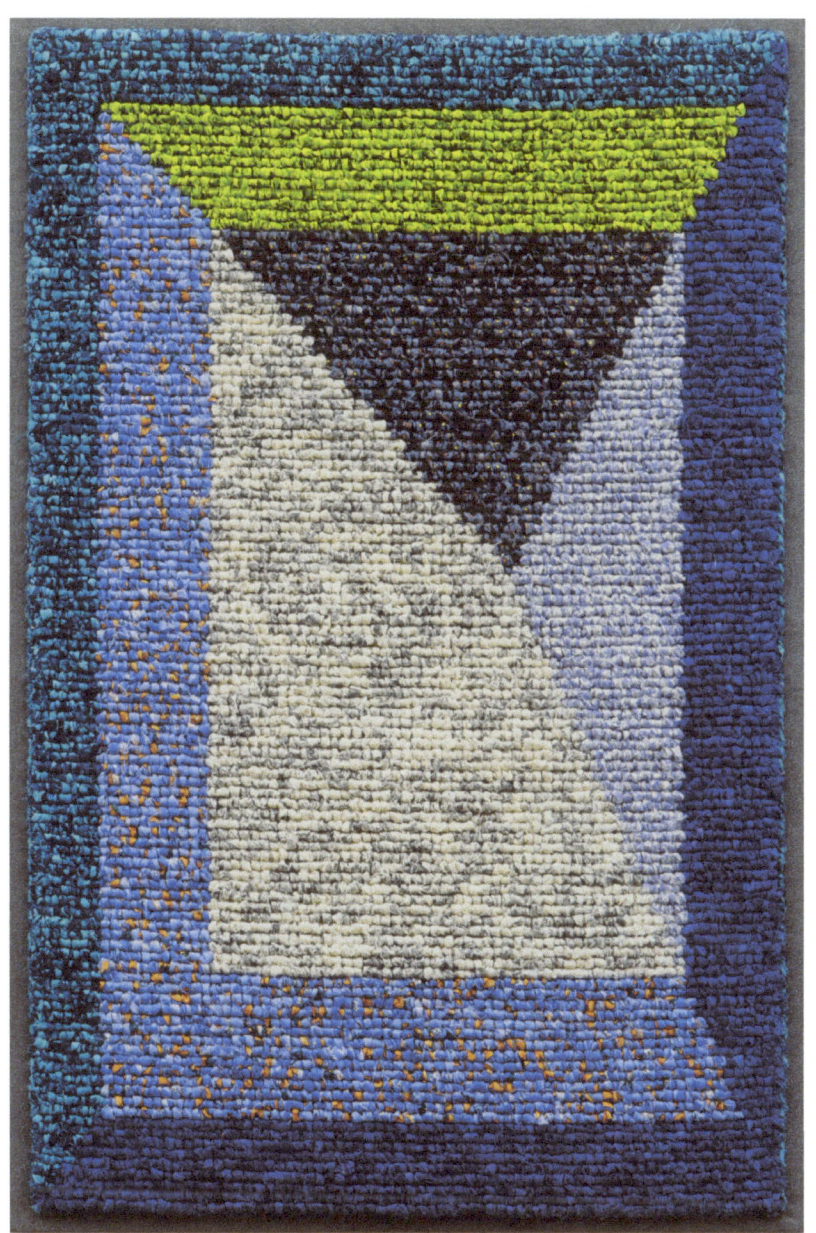

Vanishing Point 4   cotton and linen   31"x21"   2007

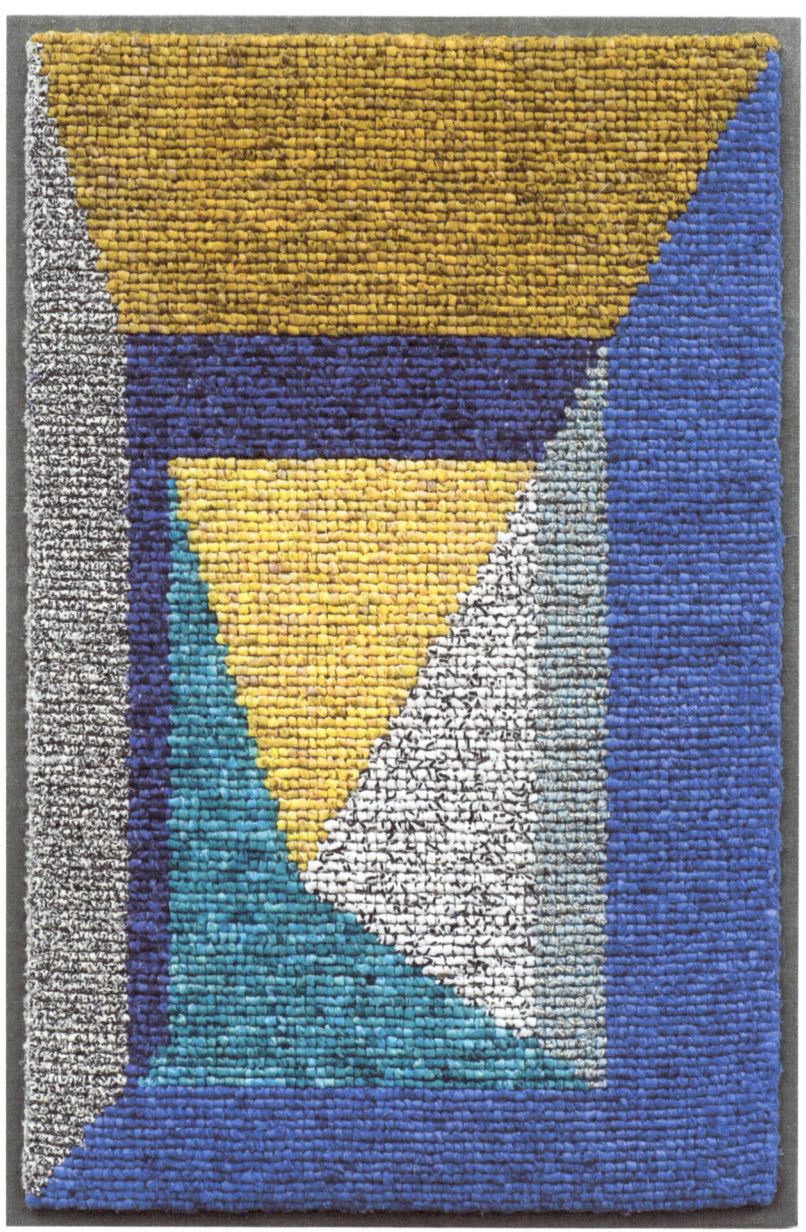

Vanishing Point 5   cotton and linen   31"x21"   2007

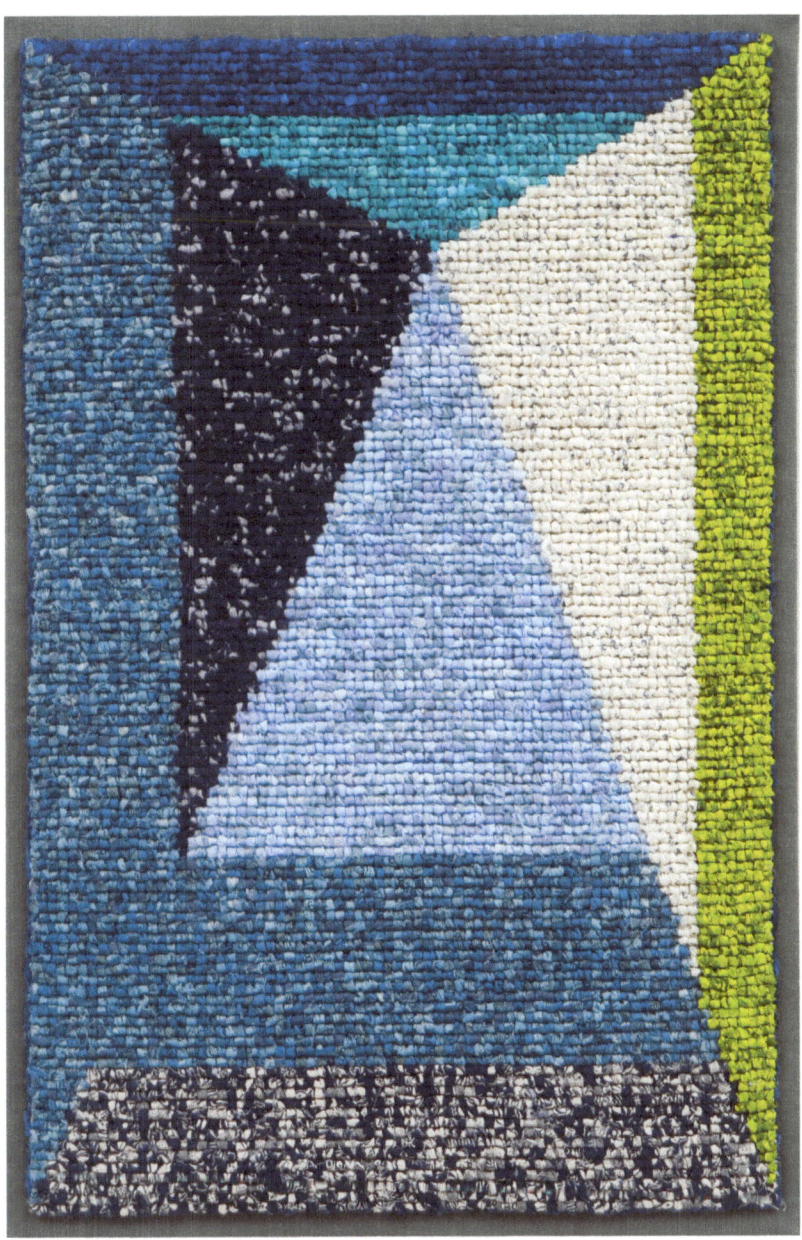

Vanishing Point 6   cotton and linen   31"x21"   2007

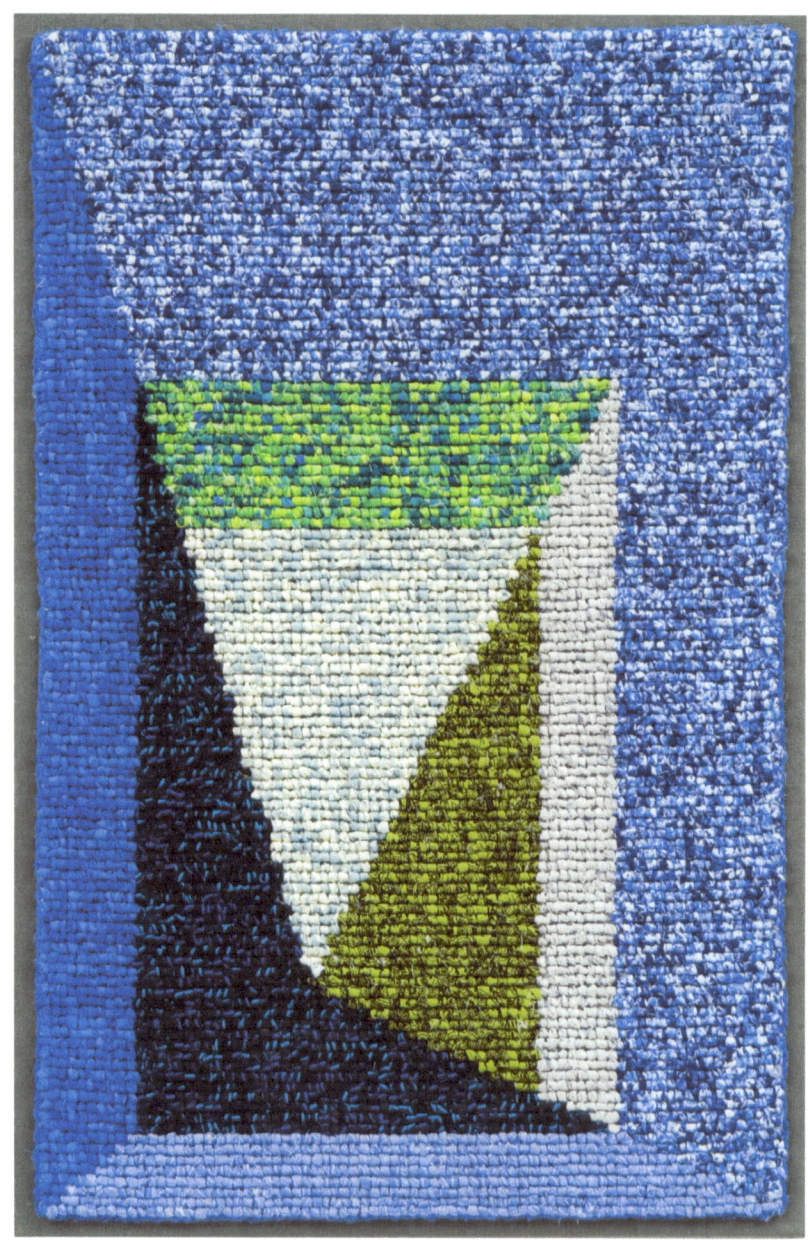

Vanishing Point 7   cotton and linen   31"x21"   2007

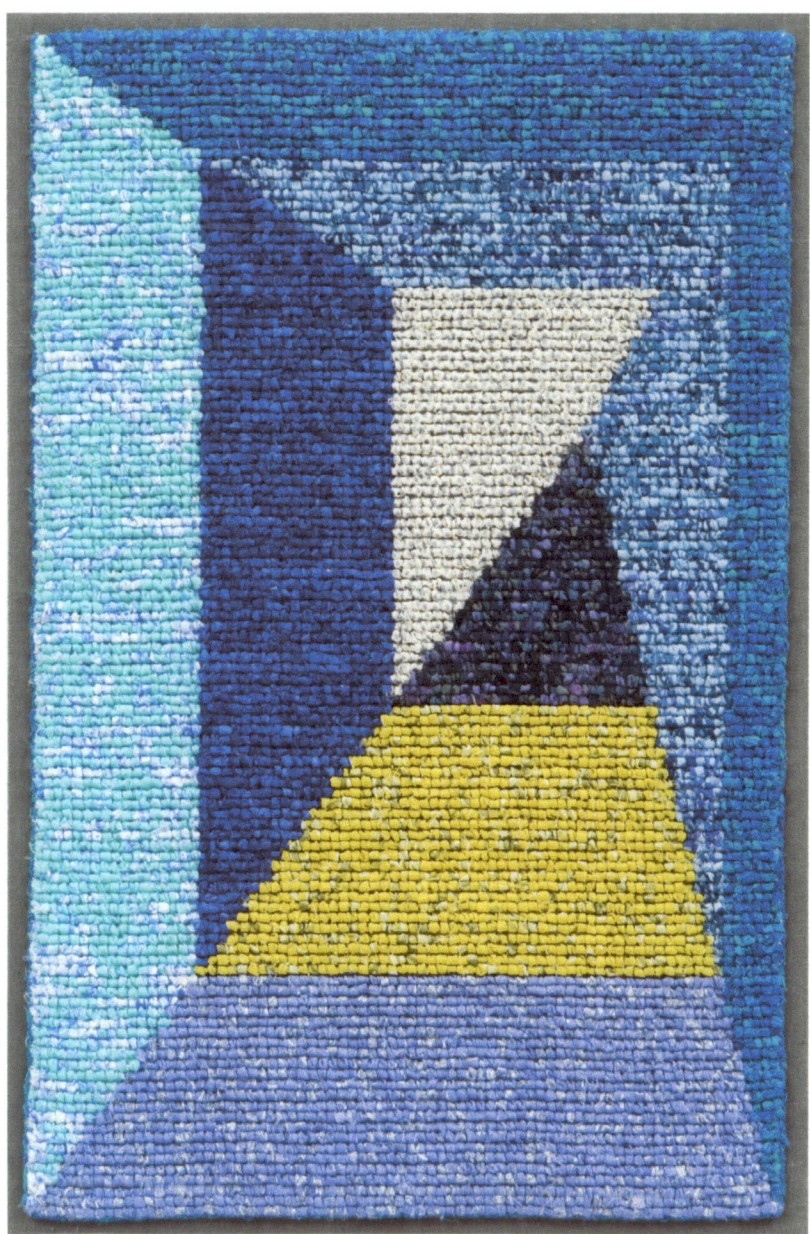

Vanishing Point 8   cotton and linen   31"x21"   2007

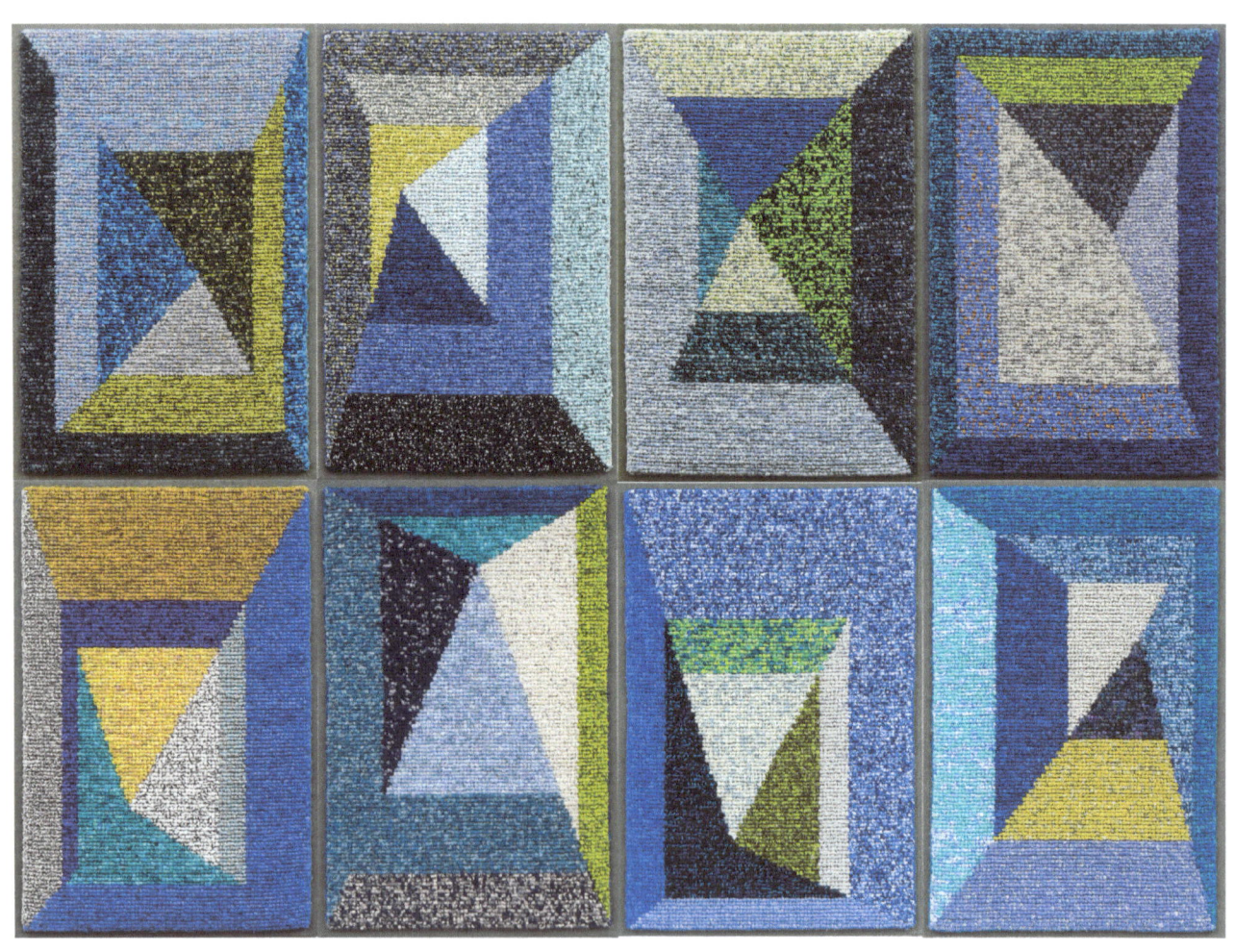

Vanishing Points 1-8   cotton and linen   eight panels, each 31"x21"   2007

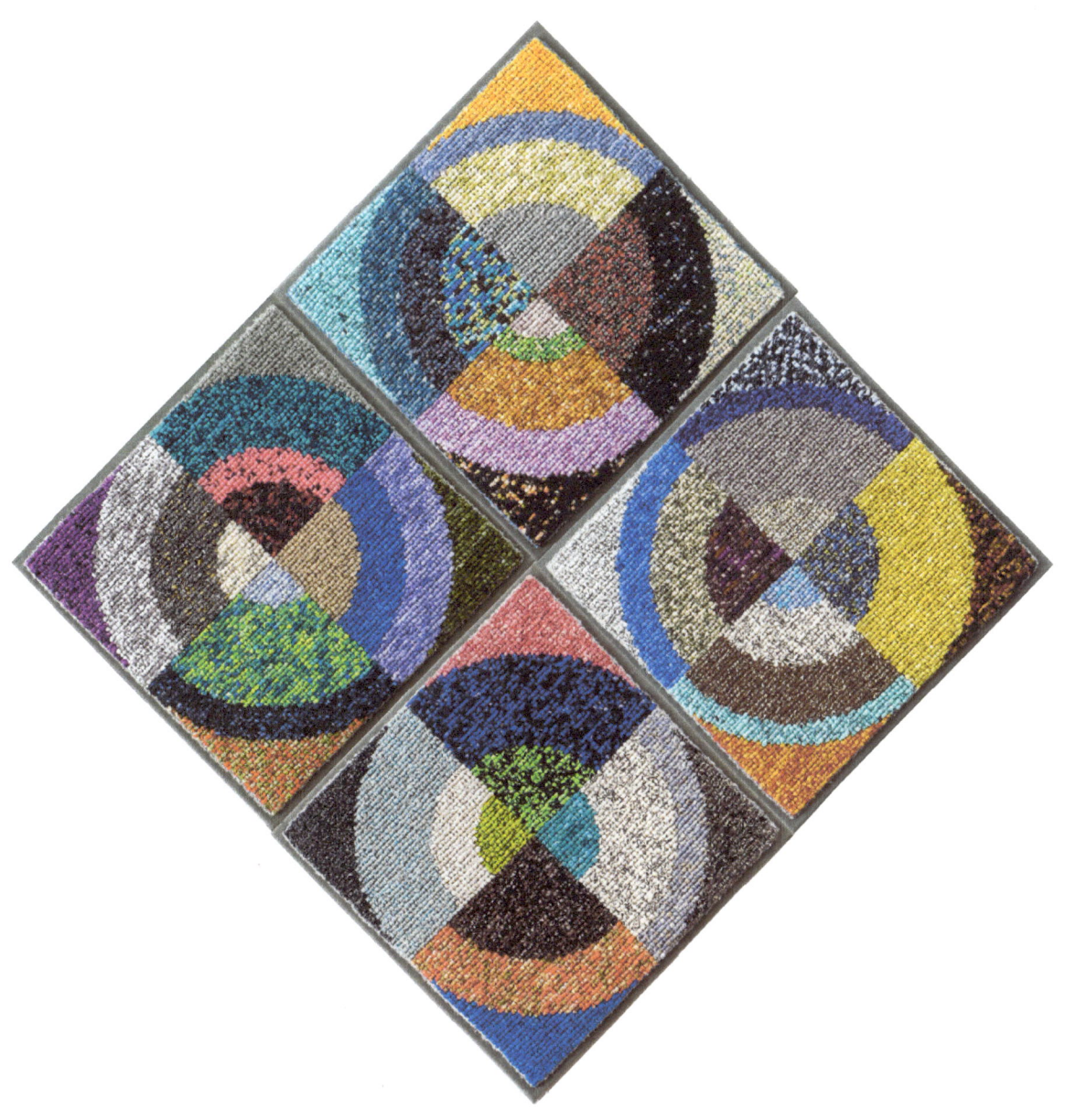

Meditations 1–4   cotton and linen   four panels, each 21"x21"   2007

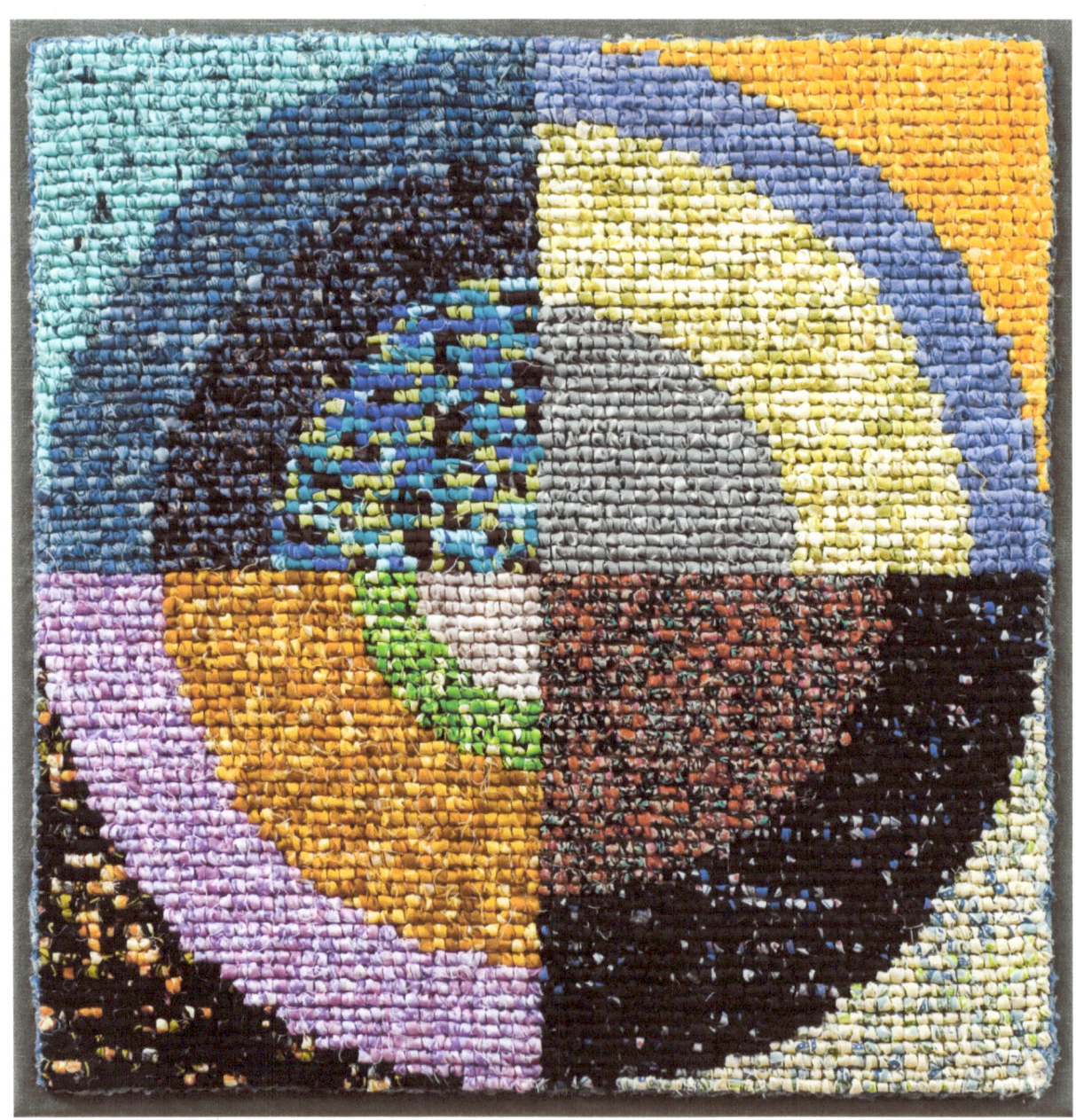

Meditation 1   cotton and linen   21"x21"   2007

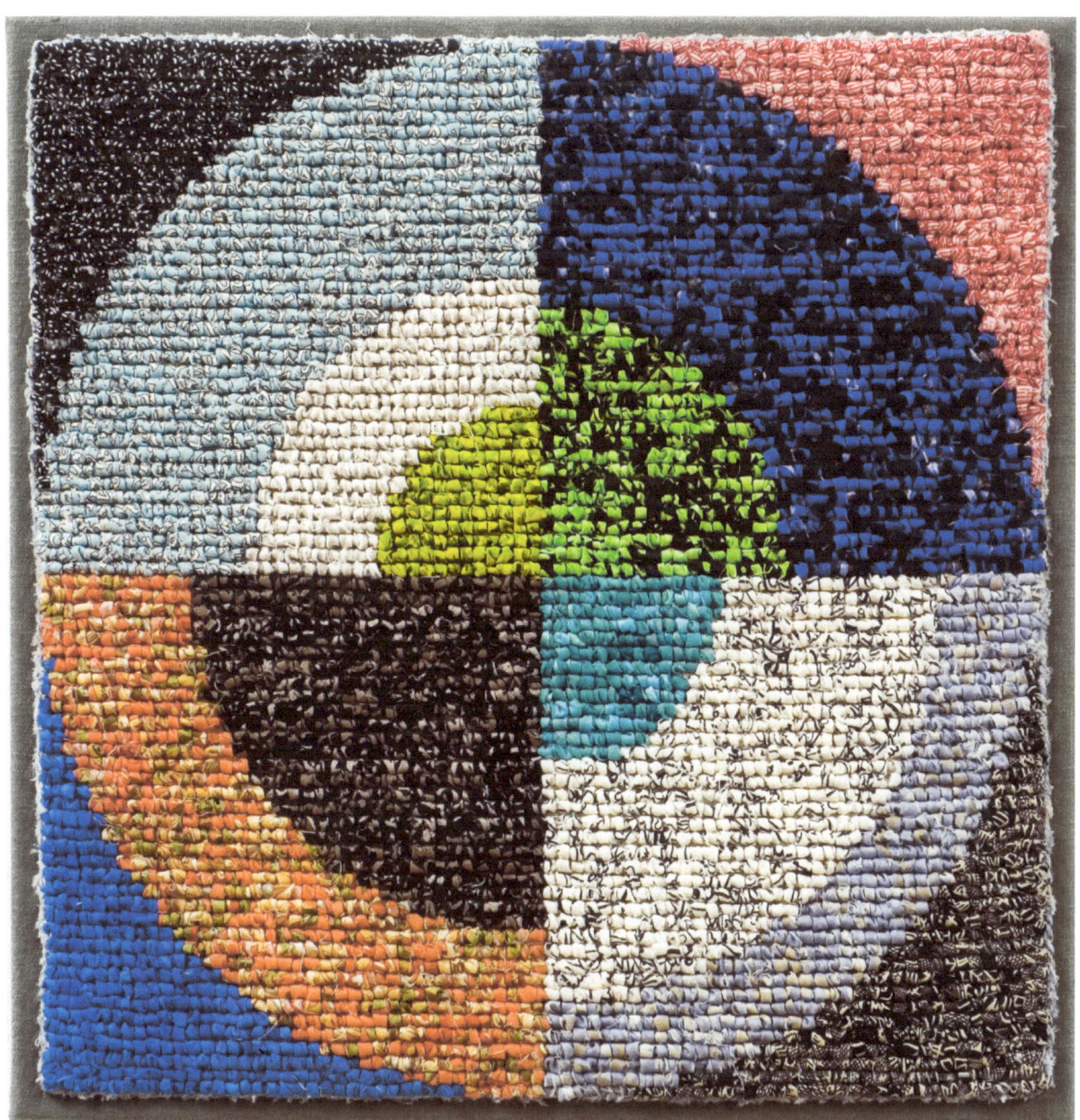

Meditation 2   cotton and linen   21"x21"   2007

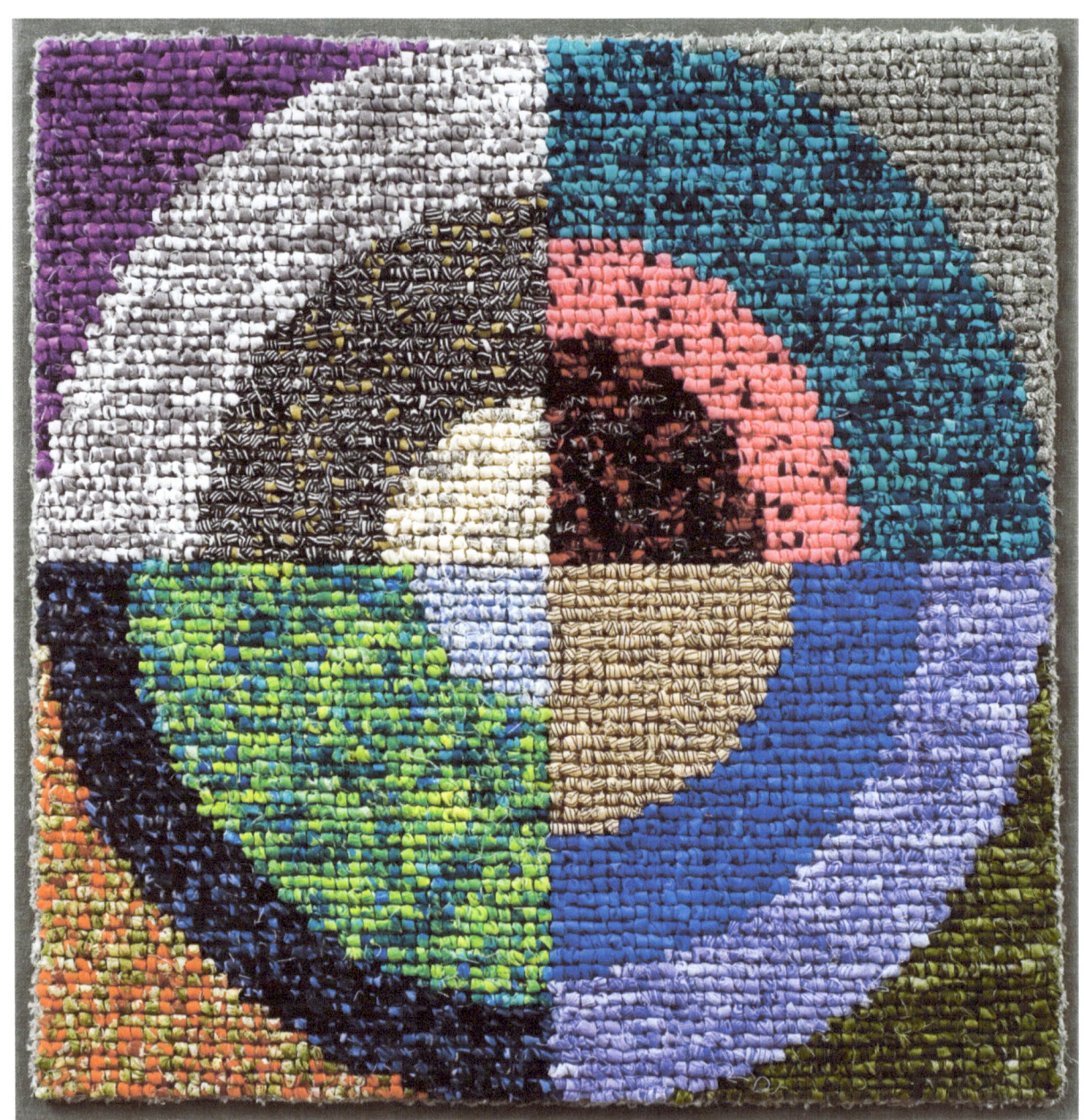

Meditation 3   cotton and linen   21"x21"   2007

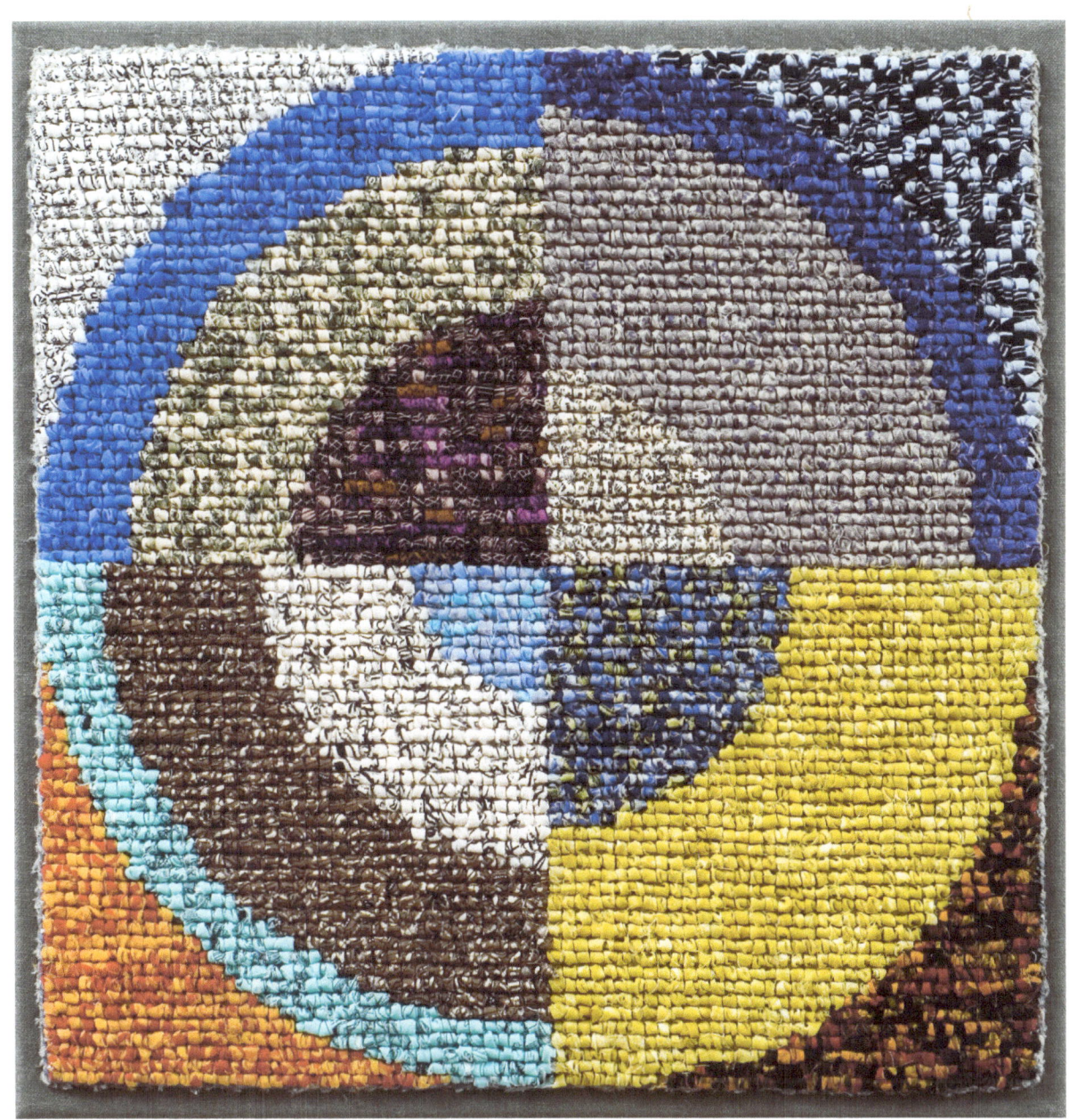

Meditation 4   cotton and linen   21"x21"   2007

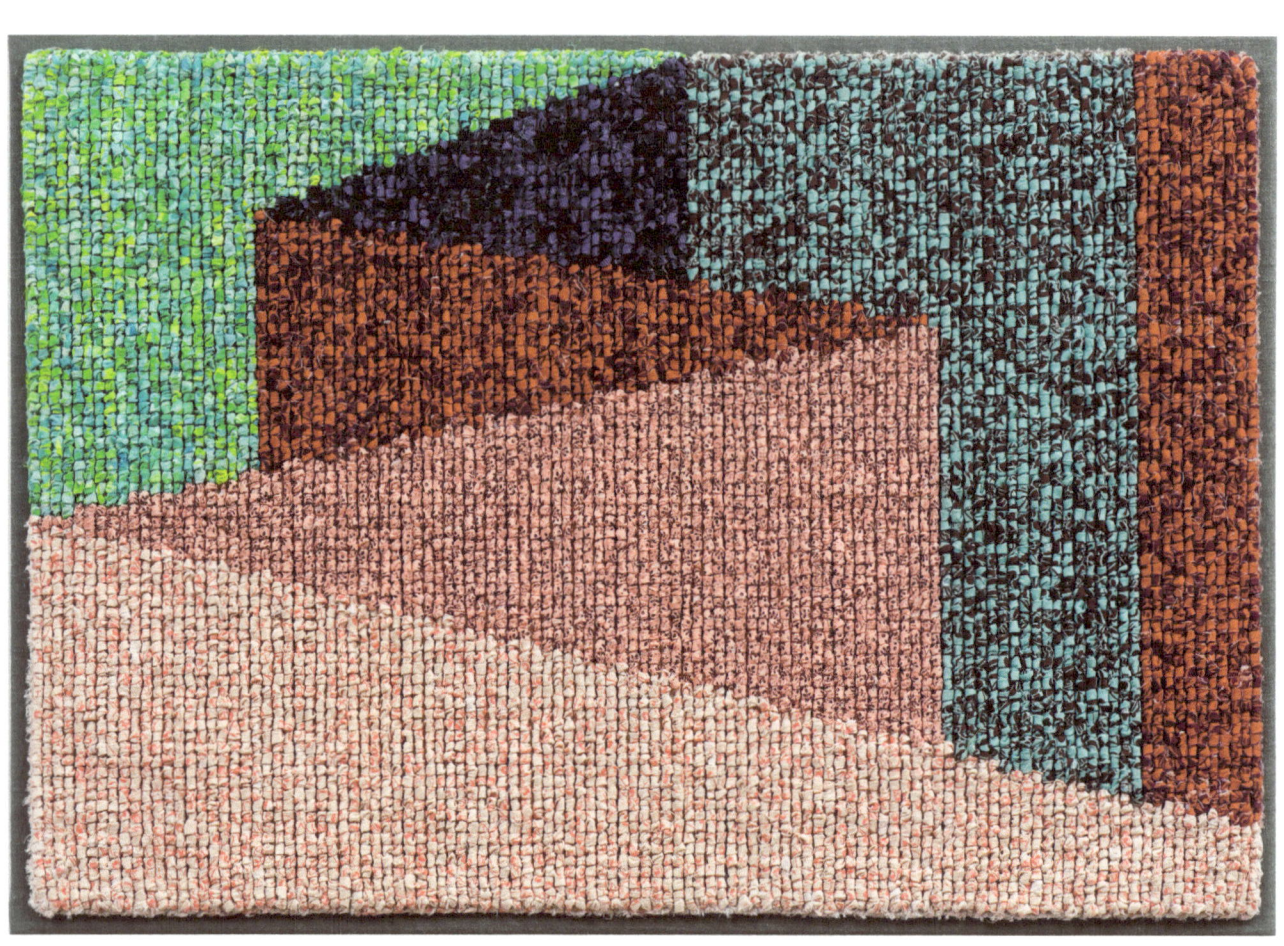

Unfolding 1   cotton and linen   31"x21"   2008

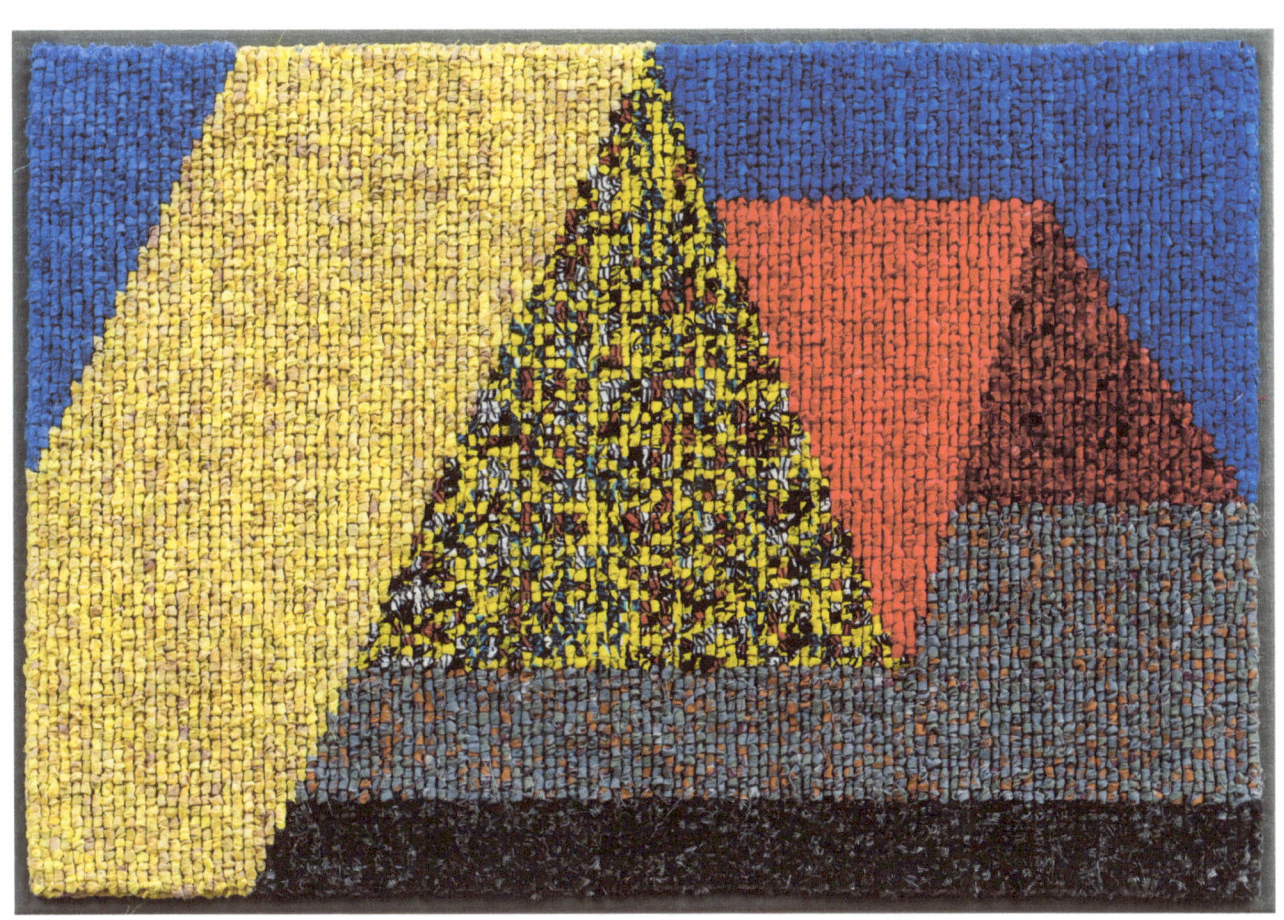

Unfolding 2   cotton and linen   31"x21"   2008

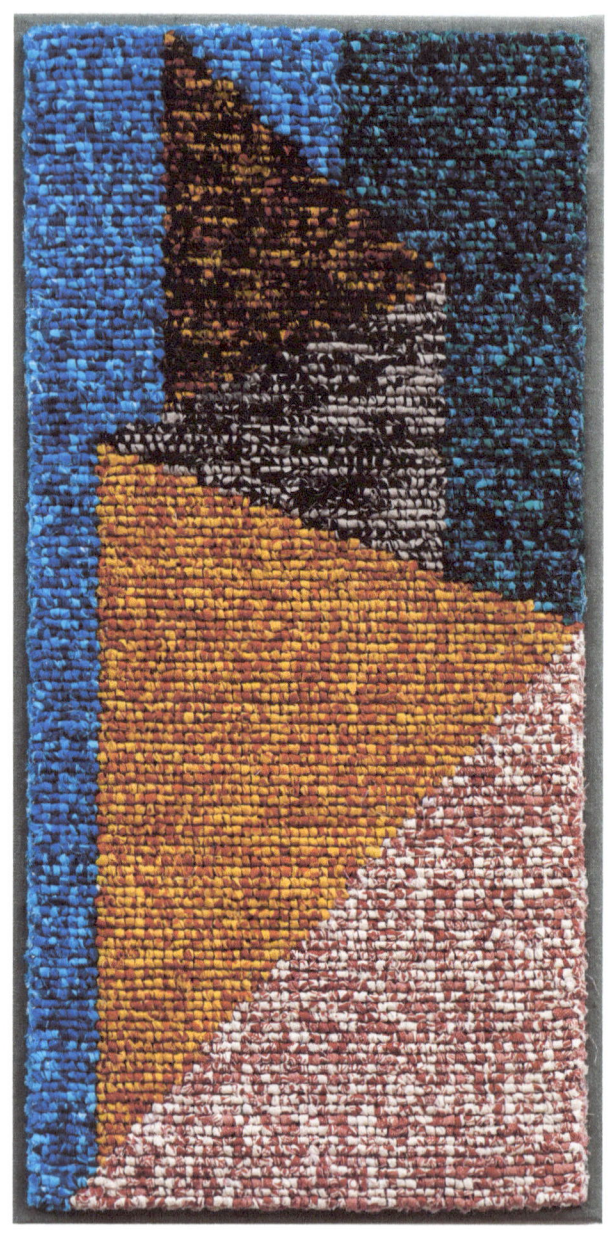

Unfolding 3   cotton and linen   31"x16"   2008

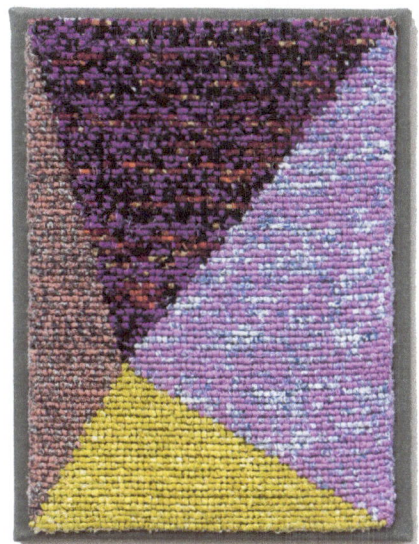 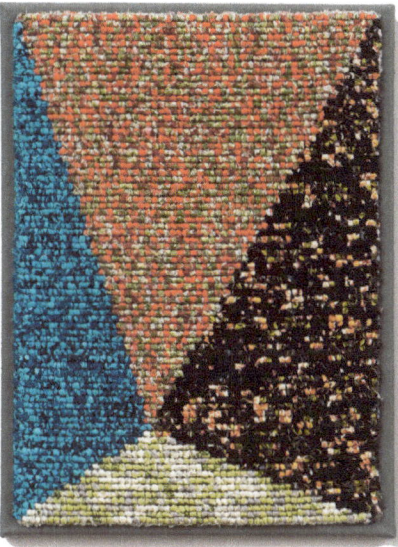 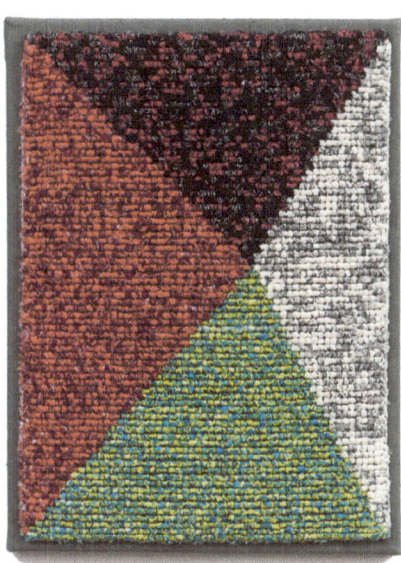

Crossroads Triptych   cotton and linen   three panels, each 21"x 16"   2008

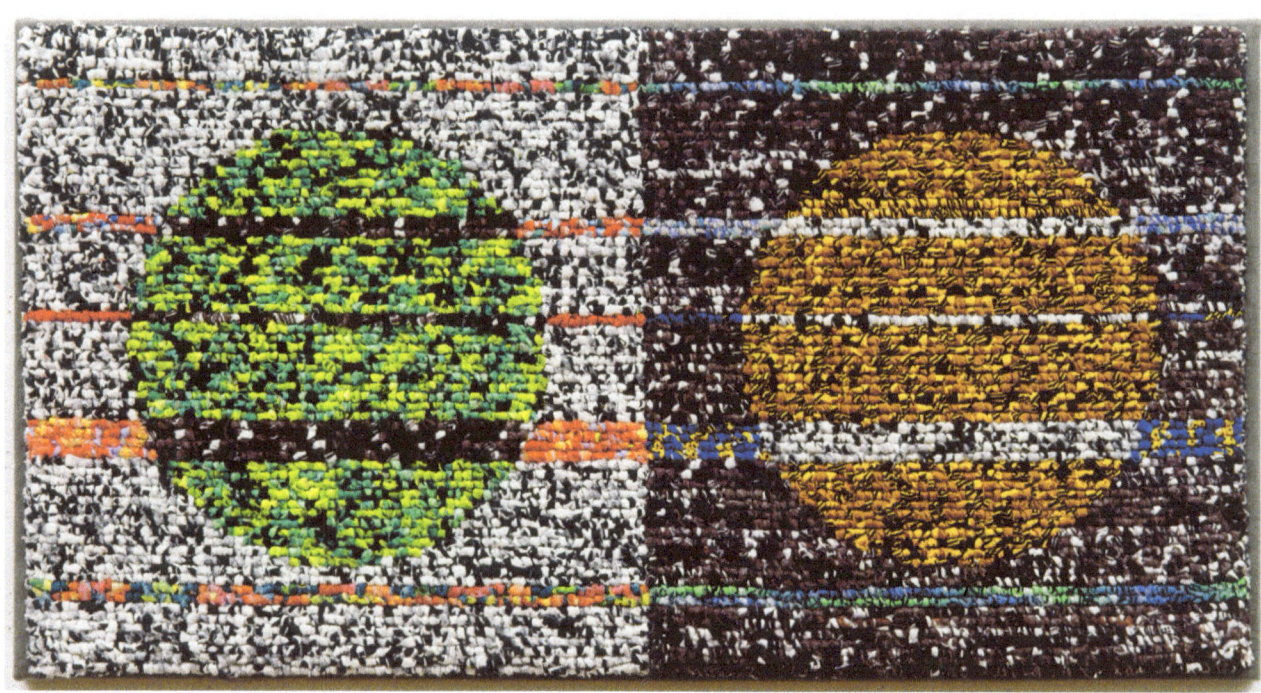

Parallel Worlds   cotton and linen   18"x35"   2007

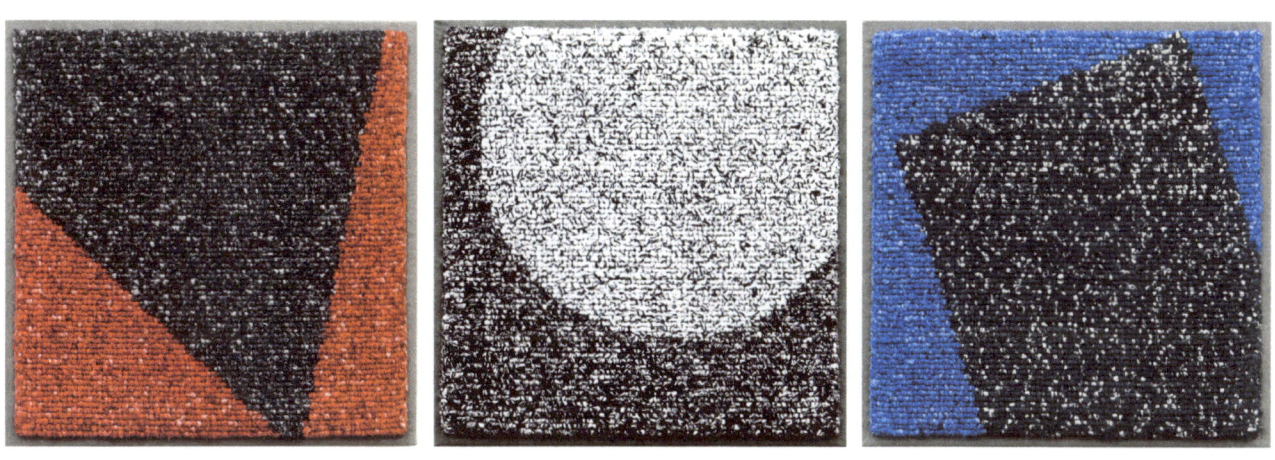

Red White & Blue   cotton and linen   three panels, each 21"x21"   2007

MARILYN HENRION

SELECTED SOLO EXHIBITIONS

2008 Noho Gallery, New York, NY
2006 Noho Gallery, New York, NY
     Galerie Gora, Montreal, Quebec, Canada
2005 Treasure Room Gallery, The Interchurch
     Center, New York, NY
2004 Noho Gallery, New York, NY
2002 Noho Gallery, New York, NY
2001 Thirteen Moons Gallery, Santa Fe, NM
2000 Noho Gallery, New York, NY
1997 Decouvrir Gallery, Seattle, WA
     Atlantic Community College Gallery,
     Mays Landing, NJ
1996 American Association for the
     Advancement of Science, Wash., DC
1994 Merrill Lynch Corporate Art Gallery,
     Plainsborough, NJ
1992 Educational Testing Corporation Art
     Gallery, Princeton, NJ

SELECTED GROUP EXHIBITIONS

2008 Columbus Museum of Art, Columbus, OH,
     Material Matters
2007 Pen & Brush Gallery, New York, NY
     Award Winners Exhibition
2006 Ross Art Museum, Delaware, OH, The
     Essence of Things
2005 Carl Solway Gallery, Cincinnatti, OH,
     BEYOND TRADITION
2005 Center for Visual Arts, Denton, TX
     Materials Hard & Soft
2004 American Textile History Museum,
     Lowell, MA, Art Quilts from the
     Collection of the Museum of Arts &
     Design
2001 Longview Art Museum, Longview, TX,
     Quilts: A Journey Through History
2000 Pavillion Josephine, Strasbourg, France,
     Art Quilts: America At The Millenium
1999 New York State Museum, Albany, NY
     Contemporary Crafts of New York State
     American Craft Museum, New York, NY
     9x9x3
1996 Museum of Decorative & Applied Arts,
     Moscow, Russia, Five Perspectives:
     American Art Quilts

SELECTED COLLECTIONS

Museum of Arts & Design, New York, NY
AQS Museum, Paducah, KY
U.S. Embassy, Pnom Penh, Cambodia
Dana Farber Cancer Institute, Boston, MA
Carnegie Abbey Country Club, Portsmouth, RI
SAS Institute Inc., Cary, NC
Avaya Communuications, Denver, CO
Lucent Technologies, Denver, CO
Kaiser Permanente, Denver, CO

Valley Hospital, Ridgewood, NJ
Rodale Press, Emmaus, PA
St. Rita Medical Center, Lima, OH
Comanche Cty. Medical Center, Lawton, OK
Rodale Press, Emmaus, PA
Nihon Vogue, Tokyo, Japan
Smithsonian Institution Archives of American Art,
Washington, DC

SELECTED BIBLIOGRAPHY

Lenkowsky, Kate, "Contemporary Art Quilts",
Indiana University Press, 2008
Atkins, Jacqueline, "Quilting Transformed: Leaders
In Contemporary Qiuilting in the U.S.-The 20th
Century & Beyond", Nihon Vogue, Tokyo, 2007
Walenti, Joseph, "New York Views", Abstract Art
Online, 10/06
"Geometry Unmoored", Disturbances, catalog, '06
McCormack, Ed, "Inner & Outer Horizons in the
Art of Marilyn Henrion", Gallery & Studio, 6/04
Sider, Sandra, "Folk Art Aesthetics and American
Art Quilts" FIBERARTS, 11/03
McCormack, Ed, "Marilyn Henrion's Ultimate
Triumph", Gallery & Studio, 12/03
Kirkham, Dr. Patricia, ed., "Women Designers In The
U.S.A. 1900-2000", Yale Univ. Press, 11/00
Steiner, Raymond J., "Marilyn Henrion at Noho
Gallery", Art Times Journal, 1/03
Neuman, Ursula, "Quilts From Six Continents: The
American Craft Museum Collection" catalog, 2002
Martin, Lois, "Timeless Moments: Marilyn Henrion",
Surface Design Journal, Winter, 2001

Sider, Sandra, "Marilyn Henrion: Art Quilts That
Pulsate With Energy", FIBERARTS, 3/01
Eaton, J. Sanders, "Tradition & Innovation in the
Art of Marilyn Henrion, Gallery & Studio, 6/00
Shaw, Robert, The Art Quilt", Hugh Lauter
Levin, pub., 1997
Fargetton, Brigitte, "Geometrie et Sensibilitie", Les
Nouvelles du Patchwork, France, 6/97
Freudenheim, Betty, "Brilliance In Color & Pattern",
New York Times, 4/94
Ishakawa, Naomi, "The Quilts of Marilyn Henrion",
Patchwork Tsushin, Japan, 4/94
Fargetton, Brigitte, "Les Poemes en Tissus de
Marilyn Henrion", Les Nouvelles du Patchwork,
France, 4/94
Freudenheim, Betty, "Quilts Composed As Poems
In Cloth", New York Times, 3/1/92

AWARDS

2005 New York Foundation for the Arts
Fellowship
2003 Brisons Veor Trust Fellowship
1999 New york State Crafts Alliance Grant
1997 Friends of Fiber Art International Grant
1995/6 Artslink Foundation Fellowship Grant

EDUCATION

1952 The Cooper Union College of Arts &
Sciences, Third Year Certificate
1972 Fordham University, Bachelor of Arts

www.ingramcontent.com/pod-product-compliance
Lightning Source LLC
Chambersburg PA
CBHW051104180526
45172CB00002B/770